Edison on Innovation

Edison on Innovation

102 Lessons in Creativity for Business and Beyond

Alan Axelrod

JOSSEY-BASS
A Wiley Imprint
www.josseybass.com

Published by Jossey-Bass
A Wiley Imprint
989 Market Street, San Francisco, CA 94103-1741—www.josseybass.com

Readers should be aware that Internet Web sites offered as citations and/or sources for further
information may have changed or disappeared between the time this was written and when it
is read.

Limit of Liability/Disclaimer of Warranty: While the publisher and author have used their
best efforts in preparing this book, they make no representations or warranties with respect
to the accuracy or completeness of the contents of this book and specifically disclaim any
implied warranties of merchantability or fitness for a particular purpose. No warranty may
be created or extended by sales representatives or written sales materials. The advice and
strategies contained herein may not be suitable for your situation. You should consult with a
professional where appropriate. Neither the publisher nor author shall be liable for any loss
of profit or any other commercial damages, including but not limited to special, incidental,
consequential, or other damages.

Jossey-Bass books and products are available through most bookstores. To contact Jossey-Bass
directly call our Customer Care Department within the U.S. at 800-956-7739, outside the
U.S. at 317-572-3986, or fax 317-572-4002.

Jossey-Bass also publishes its books in a variety of electronic formats. Some content that
appears in print may not be available in electronic books.

Library of Congress Cataloging-in-Publication Data

Axelrod, Alan.
    Edison on innovation : 102 lessons in creativity for business and beyond / Alan Axelrod.
      p. cm.
  Includes bibliographical references and index.
    ISBN 978-0-7879-9459-4 (cloth)
      1. Creative ability in business. 2. Technological innovations. 3. Management.
  4. Edison, Thomas A. (Thomas Alva), 1847–1931. I. Title.
  HD53.A985   2008
  658.4'063—dc22

                                             2007040906

Printed in the United States of America
FIRST EDITION
HB Printing   10 9 8 7 6 5 4 3 2 1

For Anita and Ian

Contents

Preface

He had more than a thousand patents to his name, including those for electric lighting, electric power generation, the phonograph, the basics of movie making, and even wax paper. If Edison wasn't a genius, who was, is, or could ever be?

There is no question that Thomas Alva Edison was and remains the name-brand marquee inventive genius—a "modern Prometheus" no less or, at the very least, the "Wizard of Menlo Park." And for us nongeniuses, that is precisely the problem. Real geniuses may create any number of wonderful things, but otherwise they're really of no use to the rest of us. What can we even pretend to learn from them?

Imitate Beethoven. Think like Einstein.

Could any advice be more useless? Such people are made of different stuff from the rest of us. If we could "be like" them, we would be one of them.

When I first began thinking about this book, I wanted to call it *Edison Was No Genius*. The title and the idea came to me while I was engaged in 2005 as a consultant on creativity and leadership training by The Henry Ford, the famous museum and collection of historical buildings (including one of Edison's workshops) founded by Henry Ford in Dearborn, Michigan. The professional staff of The Henry Ford was pondering the feasibility of establishing a program of creativity training seminars for key leaders of American industry. The question the staff posed was this: Could the institution's unparalleled collection of the artifacts and records of technological innovation be used effectively to teach others to be innovative in a focused and consistently productive way?

The answer, I said, was yes, and I began to think of *Edison Was No Genius* as a set of cases in point. The book soon evolved into *Edison on Innovation*, and its principal thesis is an invitation to all readers to consider the inventor not as a demigod from Olympus, a being apart, a divinely gifted lucky stiff, but as one of us, different in degree, to be sure, but not in kind.

What is the value of seeing Edison this way? Certainly not to diminish him, but to transform our perception of him from a figure for dumbstruck admiration into an example for practical emulation. And why emulate Edison?

First: Based on the evidence of his 1,093 patents, some of them at the heart of modern civilization, I can think of no more creative human being on the planet.

And second: Because he *can* be emulated. As will be explained in "Lesson 1: Stop Thinking and Act Like a Genius," the historical record is sufficiently extensive, detailed, and accessible to provide a clear picture of Edison's creative method. Based on this picture, *Edison on Innovation* formulates and presents 102 "lessons" in creativity.

This volume is not a biography of Thomas Edison but a book for inventors and for innovators of all sorts. It is, in fact, a book for anyone who needs or wants to be creative—on demand, practically anywhere, practically anytime. The truth is that most of us, most of the time, feel as remote and removed from creativity as we do from genius. We believe that creativity, like genius, is something that just happens, not something we can make happen. What the example of Edison demonstrates is that creativity of the very highest order can indeed be made to happen, summoned up at will, and even reduced to a reliable working method and set of principles. That method and those principles are what *Edison on Innovation* is all about, and I am confident that this introduction to Edison's creative career, creative method, and creative habits will be a revelation to anyone whose business requires the continual creation of new ideas and the practical realization of the best of them.

January 2008   Alan Axelrod
Atlanta, Georgia

Edison on Innovation

INTRODUCTION

Lesson 1: Stop Thinking and Act Like a Genius

This is what you think:

- Geniuses are born, not made.
- I was not born a genius.
- Good thing my job doesn't require me to be a genius.
- At least I make a decent living.

And you think this, too:

- Geniuses are outrageously creative.
- Creativity is spontaneous. It just happens. You can't simply turn it on like a light bulb. (Unless, of course, you're a genius.)
- Good thing I make a decent living.
- But why do I still wish I were a creative genius?

How do I know that you think these things? Because most of us think them. They are products of the myths we clutch uncritically and allow our lives to be guided by.

Doubtless, some myths produce useful ideas. But the thoughts listed here are just so much excess and burdensome baggage that holds nothing of use and just drags us back. So why not lay these burdens down? Don't worry about whether the ideas are true or not. Just put them down and walk away. True or false, they're so much dead weight.

Let's take the heaviest one first: *Geniuses are born, not made.* (Almost certainly true.)

Next? *I was not born a genius.* (You're probably right.)

Good thing my job doesn't require me to be a genius. I make a decent living. (Lucky you.)

Geniuses are outrageously creative. (No argument here.)

Creativity is spontaneous. It just happens. You can't simply turn it on like a light bulb. (Wrong!)

And I have the case in point to prove it wrong: the career of Thomas Alva Edison, the man who invented the incandescent electric light, the electric power industry, the phonograph, the modern telephone transmitter and receiver, the movies, and, along the way, wax paper and a new, more profitable process for making Portland (artificial) cement. Educated through a few grades of elementary school, Edison practically invented modern life with a steady stream of life-altering, civilization-building devices.

Your Next Thought

That brings me to your next thought: *Look, I'm no Thomas Edison!*

But, then, Edison was no genius. He just acted like one.

The sum of his work was genius, but Edison himself was pretty ordinary. Not born a genius, he figured out ways to invent the products of genius nevertheless. Unable or unwilling to rely on the lottery of spontaneous creativity, he devised methods to turn on creativity—well, like a light bulb—whenever he needed it. And because his job really *did* require genius, and because he wasn't satisfied with making nothing more than a "decent" living, Edison needed to be creative all of the time. Outrageously so.

Thomas Alva Edison personally secured 1,093 patents between 1868 and 1931 (the year he died), an average of seventeen inventions each year for sixty-three years. No one has broken that record. Judged strictly by the numbers, perhaps no one has ever been more productively creative than Edison. And it isn't just a matter of numbers. Edison invented a technology that created a new reality in the built environment of humankind.

What can we say? It's amazing. But almost equally amazing is that we possess the information to analyze the creation of this life-altering system, all the way from inspiration to invention to commercialization and to production. In contrast to many other creators, Edison worked, as it were, in the open. He kept diaries. He wrote memos of instruction, ensuring that his small army of assistants was always in the loop. A canny self-publicist, he talked to reporters, and he talked to them a lot. Moreover, a small and dedicated army of Edison scholars has studied and commented on his life of innovation, often piecing together the series of insights, experiments, failures, and successes that added up to a particular invention. With all this information available, we can recover, reconstruct, and study the process by which he created. As he said, 99 percent of that process was visible work—systematic work, simultaneously intense yet broadly encompassing in focus. But even the 1 percent that, in most other creators, is locked in the impenetrable black box we call *inspiration* was, in the case of Edison, often clearly exposed to view.

There was a time when youngsters (as they used to be called) read the lives of presidents, generals, and other leaders with the object of learning from their achievements. This kind of preparatory reading went out of fashion a long time ago. Today, it even seems quaint, naive, corny, pretentious, or just plain hopeless to think that we could possibly learn from the likes of Alexander the Great, Napoleon, Washington, Lincoln—or Edison.

What a terrible waste to ignore all that the best of us have to teach. Despite earning a decent living, do you want to work better? Smarter? More creatively? You can bemoan the accident of birth that did not make you a creative genius. You can wish for the winning lottery number of random inspiration. You can read a stack of self-help books. Or you can look to the experience of the most creative people who have ever lived.

Your boss or your biggest client can give few directives less likely to produce creative results than the command to be creative. It is not surprising that most of us find the prospect of creativity intimidating, let alone the thought of being ordered to render creativity on demand. Creation, after all, is the province of God— and, also, of a few fortunate geniuses. Both God and the genius, most of us believe, can and do create something out of nothing. Think of Genesis, sentence number one: "In the beginning *God* created . . ."

Creating something from nothing is without question a very tall order, and the truth is, nobody can do it, not even a genius. Certainly Thomas Edison never did it, and he was one of the most creative people in all of history.

One great thing the experience of Edison teaches us is that creators always start with something, never nothing. This means, quite simply, that creativity isn't as hard as it looks. I'll prove it in the lessons that follow, each of which looks into the mind and over the shoulder of Thomas Alva Edison, an ordinary man who was extraordinarily inventive.

The first chapter of this book is a biographical sketch, but this book is not a biography. Nor is it an "inspirational story," and it is not a compendium of mottoes or maxims or rules. Rather, it is a set of exemplary lessons on creativity intended to teach an ordinary person to build extraordinary things out of ordinary materials.

Add to Thomas Edison's 1,093 inventions the one he did not patent. It may be the most useful of all: *an outrageously productive process of creativity*. And because the inventor left it in the public domain, we are free to disassemble it, take it apart, lay it all out, find out just how it works, reverse engineer it. You're not a born genius? Why not just act like one? Here's how.

1

LIFE STORY OF A
MIDDLE AMERICAN

Thomas Alva Edison was born in 1847 in the up-and-coming Ohio town of Milan. When he was six, he and his family moved to Port Huron, Michigan, another Midwestern village just entering the first flush of a prosperity born of vigorous commerce with the rest of the country, to which it was linked by the Grand Trunk Western Railway via the industrial metropolis of Detroit, which in turn communicated by lake to all the wide world beyond.

Popular culture, including a host of Horatio Alger–style juvenile biographies and two enduring film classics, *Young Tom Edison* (with Mickey Rooney in the title role) and *Edison the Man* (starring Spencer Tracy)—both released in 1940—have portrayed the inventor as a maverick child whose budding genius was both exceptional and utterly misunderstood, presaging an adult destined to blossom into a lone-wolf inventor, a creative genius who amply deserved the titles of "wizard" and "modern Prometheus."

Yet the fact was that Edison's boyhood was not at all unusual for his time and place. He was intensely curious, and his curiosity sometimes got him into trouble. Boys, as they say, will be boys, and mid-nineteenth-century America was chock full of curious boys. He was bored in school, attended classes only sporadically, and left altogether after a very few years to be home schooled by his doting mother. The very same can be said of most American boys during this period, an age when children typically attended no more than a few years of elementary school and then, before hitting their teen years, entered the workforce. The luckiest ones, like Tom Edison, had capable and willing mothers who administered the bulk of their education.

Familiar, too, is the story of how the bright, ambitious twelve-year-old Edison got himself a job as a "news butcher," a concessionaire on the Grand Trunk Western Railway, purveying newspapers, magazines, candy, sandwiches, and other merchandise to passengers between Port Huron and Detroit. Employment as a news butcher was quite common for boys during the mid-nineteenth century. Now it is true that young Edison did much more than merely sell copies of the *Detroit Free Press*. He started writing, editing, and printing his own paper, replete with news of local interest. Was this remarkable? Of course it was. But unique? Not at all. Edison's paper was just one of a good many self-published local papers that sprang up across the country, many of them produced by youths and teenagers. Without question, Edison did introduce a startling innovation into this pattern by using a small proofing press, salvaged from the offices of the *Detroit Free Press*, to print his paper aboard the moving train. This not only increased the novelty appeal of Edison's paper, it gave the news he presented a freshness that approached real-time reporting. It also allowed the young entrepreneur to make maximum use of his travel time by running off copies in a corner of the baggage car. Later, he even cleared a space in that baggage car to accommodate both his press and a table for experiments—something doubtless no other news butcher did or even thought of doing. If there is one quality Edison was indisputably born with, it was a keen awareness of the precious scarcity of time. From a very early age, he was driven to pack every moment with productive work.

Without a doubt, Thomas Edison was an innovator from a very early age; nevertheless, he had more in common with others of his era than differences from them. Like most of his young fellow countrymen, he was intensely interested in the ongoing transportation revolution that was sweeping the nation, the burgeoning of the railroads, and the related revolution in communication technology: the telegraph. Development of both technologies was spurred by the ongoing Civil War, which brought increased demand for transportation of goods and people and for instantaneous communication, including the communication of news. Young Tom's involvement with the railroad and with the news business brought him into contact with the world of telegraphy and telegraphers, and his interest in this technology quickly meshed with his natural scientific curiosity, pointing it in the direction of electricity, technology, and invention. When he started working as a telegrapher in 1863, Edison entered a fraternity of technology-minded young men, many of whom were, if not inventors, at the very least compulsive tinkerers, never content to let an electromechanical device exist without trying their hand at improving it. Most telegraphers worth their salt devoted considerable time to modifying, personalizing, or otherwise tweaking this or that feature of the equipment they used. The teenaged Edison found himself in a culture that both nurtured and demanded innovation and the solving of technical problems, almost always hands-on and on the fly. Moreover, the demand for instantaneous communication—from person to person, business to business, and reporter to newspaper—was always outrunning the available technology. Telegraph companies were perpetually hungry for invention, and they were willing to pay for it.

After some four years working as a "tramp telegrapher"—an itinerant key operator who had built a reputation among fellow telegraphers for his facility with technical innovation—Edison returned briefly to Port Huron, then in 1868 secured the backing of a Boston businessman and moved to Boston, where he set up as a full-time inventor. At the time, Boston was a major financial center, which also offered the technological resources of great universities and their libraries. The financial climate, together with the sophisticated scientific and technological environment, launched Edison on his life's work.

His first patent was for an electric vote recorder developed in 1868. The invention was a technical success—meaning that it worked as promised—but it was a commercial failure, meaning that it failed to find a market. Edison had invented it with the intention of selling it to local, state, and federal legislative bodies, having simply assumed that these customers would welcome a quick and efficient way of recording the many votes they took in the course of their work. In fact, when Edison demonstrated the device, he discovered that the very last thing legislators wanted was a quick and efficient means of voting. They had grown accustomed to exploiting the laborious and antiquated process of the roll call vote to gain much-needed time for last-minute cajoling and the marshaling of required votes. From this initial popular failure, Edison drew a valuable lesson. He resolved from then on to determine—firsthand—the existence of a market and a need before embarking on any other invention. For him, that lesson was sufficient to turn momentary failure into lifelong success. Nothing, Edison believed, was truly a failure if you managed to learn something from it.

Even though he did not grow instantly rich from the electric vote recorder, Edison's experience with the device gave him confidence in his ability to invent and innovate, and in 1869 he moved to New York City, setting up his first formal business as a manufacturer of telegraph equipment, working primarily as a subcontractor for Western Union and other companies. Two years later, in 1871, he established his own factory and combination laboratory–workshop in Newark, New Jersey. In this year, too, he married his first wife, Mary Stilwell.

Edison's most important inventions in the field of telegraphy enabled the simultaneous transmission and reception of multiple messages over a single line—a breakthrough that instantly and cheaply multiplied the capacity of the nation's telegraph system. His first quadruplex telegraph equipment was patented in 1874, and Edison used the proceeds from this and other telegraphic inventions and innovations to buy land and to build on it his most famous laboratory–workshop complex, in then-rural Menlo Park, New Jersey.

Set well apart from the roar and distractions of the big city, Menlo Park was nevertheless close enough to Manhattan to maintain important financial and cultural ties with the center of American commerce. At Menlo Park, Edison created what must be called a technology village, a pioneering industrial research facility—perhaps the world's first dedicated full-scale research and development enterprise. Edison himself dubbed it an "invention factory," and for an increasingly news-hungry press, Menlo Park became the lair of a modern wizard, a nineteenth-century Prometheus, who delivered to the world, with remarkable regularity, one technological wonder after another. The phonograph emerged in 1877, the year that also saw the creation of the carbon button transmitter, which, when perfected, would transform the Bell telephone into a truly commercial, reliable, and robust communications instrument, a device that quickly became indispensable to the modern world. In 1879, Edison demonstrated the first successful and durable electric incandescent lighting system, which included not only the incandescent lamps themselves but a fully developed system for generating, distributing, regulating, measuring, and retailing electric power. In short, Edison invented and innovated a new industry—the electric power utility—which forever changed the course of civilization. By 1882, he went to work on the electrification of lower Manhattan.

In 1884, Mary Edison died suddenly, and two years later Edison married his second wife, Mina Miller. A year after his wedding, in 1887, he built and moved into a larger laboratory–workshop–manufacturing complex in West Orange, New Jersey. Here, in 1888, he made extensive improvements on the phonograph, laboriously transforming it from a charming curiosity into a commercial product of enormous influence and profitability. In 1889, he formed Edison General Electric, then went on to create the kinetograph, an early motion picture camera. It was not until 1894 that he paired the kinetograph with the kinetoscope, a motion picture peephole-type viewer, opening up the first commercial motion picture exhibition "parlor" in New York City later in the year.

This recitation of major inventions leaves out Edison's very nearly continuous stream of minor inventions and innovations, many of them extremely profitable, adding up, before the end of the inventor's life in 1931, to 1,093 patents—a record no other individual has ever come close to equaling, let alone breaking. There were, in this remarkable career of invention and innovation, technical and commercial failures, of course, the costliest of which was a decade-long effort to develop a commercially viable process for electromagnetically separating iron from cheap low-grade ore. Likewise, Edison's efforts, early in the twentieth century, to develop a more reliable and practical storage battery to power electric vehicles were threatened by the remarkably rapid demise of electric car technology after Henry Ford successfully marketed his mass-produced Model T in 1908, thereby ensuring the triumph of the internal combustion automobile fueled by gasoline. In typical Edison fashion, the inventor recovered from both disasters. He managed to convert much of his capital investment in the ore-separating enterprise—especially his heavy machinery—into an advanced plant for the manufacture of Portland cement, and when his intended market for the storage battery crumbled away, he innovated a host of new applications for his improved storage battery, ranging from powering railway signals to providing lighting for houses and businesses isolated from the very electric lines his power technology was in the process of laying or stringing.

Edison never stopped inventing. At the very end of his life, he was researching a process for commercially extracting rubber from goldenrod, in the hope of providing a cheap and plentiful domestic source of rubber for industry, especially the burgeoning automobile industry. The scope of his interests and his practical innovations is staggering—everything from electric light to artificial cement—yet his single most important invention was never patented or embodied in a single device. It was the notion of creating and operating an "invention factory": a set of methods and practices aimed at freeing up and stimulating the creative imagination even as it harnessed that imagination in a reliable, regular, businesslike way. Edison invented the modern discipline of industrial research and development, a means of making creativity, invention—genius itself—so predictable and reliable that it could be summoned on demand, with regularity, to conceive, develop, produce, and market one technological breakthrough after another.

2

GETTING YOUR HANDS DIRTY

Lesson 2: Experiment with Everything

A number of entries in Thomas Edison's diary during the mid-1880s suggest that he was plagued by chronic indigestion. This drove him, one day, while headed to the office of the Edison Electric Light Company at 65 Fifth Avenue in New York City, to get off the streetcar at Broadway, far from his office door. "Tried experiment of walking two miles to our office," he recorded on July 13, 1885, "with idea it would alleviate my dyspeptic pains." The expedient, exercise, was hardly original as a remedy for indigestion, but what is significant in Edison's trial of it is the word—*experiment*—he used to describe what he was doing. Clearly, Edison viewed every attempted solution to every perceived problem—no matter how apparently casual or even trivial—as a deliberate, fully conscious experiment. Moreover, he apparently regarded every problem he encountered not as an obstacle, an annoyance, a threat, or a defeat, but as a welcoming invitation to experiment.

Did his experimental dyspepsia remedy actually work? Edison laconically recorded his results—for all experiments must include recorded results: "It didn't."

Nevertheless, Edison refused to regard the experiment as a failure. For him, no experiment that yielded knowledge could ever be called a failure. And this one taught him that a long walk was not a cure for indigestion. A very short time later, he tried another experiment. He accepted from a "Mrs. G_____" some "Tulu gum," conceiving (he recorded in his diary) "the idea that the mastication of this chunk of illimitable plasticity—a dentiferous tread-mill so to speak—would act on the salivial glands to produce an excess of this necessary ingredient of the digestive fluid and thus a self-acting home-made remedy for dyspepsia would be obtained." As with the two-mile walk, Edison recorded the result of this experiment as well. This time the result was more than knowledge of what did not work. He recorded, somewhat cautiously: "Believe there is something in this as my dyspeptic pains are receding from recognition."

All of us experiment all of the time—we just don't think of it in such formal terms. Experimentation is, in fact, our natural way of being in the world. You can make it more conscious and deliberate by thinking in terms of experimentation, writing down what you try, observing the results, and keeping a record of those results. At its most basic, experimentation is nothing more than trial, observation, evaluation, and recording. And no subject is too trivial a candidate for experimentation. Once acquired, the experimental habit will carry into all aspects of life, including the portion of living devoted to making a living.

Lesson 3: Become a Boy of the Nineteenth Century

Twelve-year-old Tom Edison and his father were at the railroad station, waiting for the train to take them from Milan, Ohio, where they had been visiting family, to their home in Port Huron, Michigan. They waited among a pile of crates to be shipped home to Port Huron. As a boy—and things would not be very different when he grew up—Edison found it impossible to sit still and do nothing. Spying a paint pot and brush on the platform, he marked each crate for shipment to Port Huron. The station master was so impressed by the job that he immediately offered Edison $30 a month plus room and board to work as his factotum.

That should have been job enough for any ambitious boy, but Tom Edison had what he considered a much better idea. With his father's help, he set himself up as a "news butcher" or "news butch" on the Grand Trunk Western Railway, riding the rails between Port Huron and Detroit, hawking newspapers, magazines, snacks, cigars, dime novels, joke books, and various sundries.

It was not an unusual job for a twelve-year-old boy. By the mid-nineteenth century, youthful news butchers had become regular fixtures of American rail travel. Nevertheless, Edison innovated on the job, elevating the concept of news butcher to a new height. To begin with, he resolved not to waste the long layover between his daily arrival in Detroit and the departure of the train for the return trip to Port Huron. He joined the local Young Men's Society and used his layover time to visit the society's library, from which he proceeded to give himself an education in the fundamentals of science and technology. He also became a regular at the offices of the *Detroit Free Press*—whose papers he sold on the train—and, ingratiating himself with some of the staff, obtained discarded type, ink, and paper. He borrowed or purchased from the *Free Press* a small flatbed proofing press, set it up in a corner of the train's baggage car, and began to print his own newspaper, the *Grand Trunk Herald*, en route to and from Detroit. Some stories were copied wholesale from other papers, but Edison also wrote and printed a liberal selection of original, local material. He sold the *Herald* by the copy as well as for a subscription price of 8 cents per month. His total output was twenty-four issues, printed over six months of 1862. In the heated and news-hungry climate of Civil War America, the *Herald* proved surprisingly popular with Grand Trunk passengers, who were not only eager for local news but were doubtless charmed by the novelty of reading a paper printed on a moving train.

Was this precocious in young Tom Edison? Without a doubt. But was it evidence of absolute genius? Not at all.

If the job of news butcher was a common one among youngsters of mid-nineteenth-century America, the country was also full of individuals—amateurs—who printed and sold their own newspapers. Surprisingly enough, many of these entrepreneurs were teenagers. As a boy of ambition, as an energetic and successful news butcher, and even as the writer, editor, and publisher of his own newspaper, young Tom Edison was not so much a maverick, let alone a unique genius, as he was part of an American youth movement.

Yet this did not make him a mere follower. Although he latched onto a set of going phenomena—on-train sales and amateur news publishing—he innovated elaborately upon them by introducing the novelty of printing the newspaper on board a moving train. In an age before radio, television, and the Internet, Edison was selling news very nearly in real time, and his customers found the idea most appealing. It is not surprising that, from here, Edison's next job would be as an apprentice telegrapher—a working student of the new electric technology that closed the gap between event and event report even more closely than Edison could by writing, printing, and distributing the news en route from one place to another.

> Innovation may begin by tracking a trend, but it succeeds by coming—in some significant way—to lead the very trend it originally tracked.

Lesson 4: Knowing

Contrary to popular mythology, which often portrays him as an exclusively hands-on, strictly trial-and-error experimenter, Edison did not disdain scientific theory, but he did put the very highest value on theory that was directly founded on firsthand observation based on actual experimentation. Moreover, he did not feel that he could truly know a subject if all he had was a theoretical knowledge of it. To gain the knowledge he believed necessary for the creation of an invention, Edison would begin by taking steps to understand fully the electrical or chemical properties of the elements of whatever device he was building. Concrete, specific, intimate knowledge of these properties was far more meaningful to him as an inventor and innovator than any book-learned grasp of the theory behind the device under development. For Edison, creativity was a high-touch enterprise.

> For the innovator, knowledge must not be an end in itself. Creative knowledge means knowing the potential of many things—forces, components, design elements, and so on—so that these may be combined into new or improved devices. For the inventor and innovator, knowledge is a matter of mastering the vocabulary of physical reality.

Lesson 5: See It

Given the more than a thousand patents Thomas Edison had to his name, including breakthroughs that created major modern industries and transformed civilization itself, it seems both perverse and mean-spirited to focus on the limits of his imagination. But it is those limits that reveal much of what is most useful to us—as innovators and would-be innovators—about his creative fertility.

In 1922, Edison wrote of his intense interest in the nascent field of atomic energy, but he observed that "we have not yet reached the point where this exhaustless force can be harnessed and utilized." Why not? Edison explained: "There is nothing to hang the imagination on."

In that simple declaration rests the heart of Edison's inventive creativity. Although he was an avid reader and never discounted the importance of gaining a theoretical understanding of scientific and technical principles, Thomas Edison worked even more with his senses than he did with his intellect. He had to *see* in order to imagine. Hard of hearing since his youth—and having grown progressively more deaf with each passing year of his adult life—Edison often remarked that his disability was truly a blessing, because his deafness forced him to rely all the more on his eyes.

Although electricity is invisible, its effects are not. Atomic energy, in contrast, was, in 1922, utterly incorporeal. Edison well understood that as a form of energy it could be converted into that other form known as electricity, but he had absolutely no idea how to do it. "There is nothing in sight just now," he wrote—and it is well to take the phrase "in sight" quite literally. Edison could not *see* the operation of this strange new form of energy. The very best he could hope for, as far as harnessing atomic power was concerned, was the occurrence of some random stroke of luck, the possibility that some "quite dissimilar but collateral problem" might one day "open up this field by accident." Short of this form of divine intervention, invisible and incorporeal atomic energy would remain a theoretical quantity only—at least as far as Thomas Edison was concerned.

> Play to your strengths. If you are a manager, manage others in innovation. If you are a theoretician, think innovatively. But if you are hands-on, innovate with your hands. See the work and see it through. Let it take shape under your touch.

Lesson 6: Working Bottom Up

Modern research and development operations, backed by major corporate money and staffed by academically trained scientists and engineers, characteristically approach the business of innovation and invention from the top down. That is, they begin with people who have a strong background in academic principles and a thorough grasp of theory and assign to these persons the task of looking for practical applications for the theory and principles. Having identified the potential applications, the same people are further tasked with actually creating them. At its very best, this approach can save a great deal of time by shortcutting or entirely eliminating the process of trial and error. Moving from the top down may get the initial prototype of any new device closer to its target faster.

Despite the advantages of the approach, Edison almost never worked from the top down. Instead, he naturally took a bottom-up approach, typically conceiving an idea, sketching approaches for its practical realization, and then building prototypes—which he observed, manipulated, and modified until he had fashioned a satisfactory solution to whatever problem he had defined.

Top down, bottom up: Which method is better? The answer depends on the project in question and on the creative habits of the inventors and innovators involved. The importance of the example of Edison is the revelation that the now-prevailing top-down model, which is pervasive throughout the R&D community, does not represent the only viable approach to innovation. Certainly, it is impossible to ignore Edison's creative success. This being the case, at the very least, it makes sense to consider a combination of the top-down and bottom-up approaches as a means of facilitating and accelerating invention and innovation. Consider setting as a goal the rapid movement from theory to prototypes, then work with the resulting range of prototypes to climb back up to a revision of theoretical understanding so as to create a final prototype that is spot on target.

Lesson 7: Do the Thing Itself

Popular culture, including the 1940 Mickey Rooney film *Young Tom Edison,* has made much of the budding inventor's ill luck with formal education. In fact, Edison's scant time in an elementary school classroom and his subsequent home schooling by his mother were hardly unusual in the nineteenth century. That is, Tom Edison was neither more nor less formally educated than the vast majority of American males of his era. Nevertheless, it is also true that most of Edison's education came entirely through his own efforts. He was an autodidact who devoured books, among which—by his twelfth year—was *Natural Philosophy* by a Boston high school principal named Richard Parker.

During the historical period encompassing Edison's youth, the term *natural philosophy* was a somewhat archaic but still widely used synonym for what is today called *physics*. Probably because he was writing for boys and adolescents, Parker took a homespun and real-world view rather than a formal, theoretical approach to his subject. This meant that his discussion of electricity and magnetism included many examples from recent technology, including the telegraph, a communications breakthrough so pervasive in the 1850s, when the book appeared, that Parker chose an illustration of telegraph apparatus as the frontispiece of his book.

No biography can accurately tell us what its subject *thought*, but it is often possible to know what that subject read and, by knowing this, infer the development of mind. In the case of Edison, we know that he read Parker at about the age of twelve, and we also know that, later in life, he recalled having built a half-mile telegraph line between his house and that of a friend, James Clancy, by about this age. It does not require any great stretch of imagination to assume that he used what he read in Parker to build his line. Thus his homemade telegraph system was not an act of genius but one of initiative, curiosity, willingness to work, and a taste for scientific reading matter. This said, we still must ask: How many other twelve-year-old boys built telegraph lines in the mid-nineteenth century?

Learning by doing does not demand the pristine originality of inspirational genius, but it does require *doing*, not just learning. Edison's spark was not so much divine genius as it was a sufficient fire in the belly to put his thoughts into material form, to take action on his ideas—whatever their ultimate source.

Lesson 8: Cut and Try

For Edison, creativity was always more a matter of investigative labor than of imaginative inspiration. His most famous aphorism—"Genius is 99 percent perspiration and 1 percent inspiration"—testifies to that. His creative methodology has often been described as a process of cut and try. When he was on the hunt for the ideal filament for his electric lamp, he collected a sample of every conceivable substance that could possibly be formed into a filament, and he tried each, recording the results of thousands of observations. There were few theoretical shortcuts in this process. Whatever worked worked. Whatever did not did not. And once something was found to work, Edison might use it—but he would rarely stop looking for something that worked even better.

Cutting and trying was labor-intensive, to be sure, but careful observation and record keeping allowed Edison to compile a vast compendium of the physical and chemical properties of a staggering array of substances. Thus the time devoted to finding the best filament for the electric lamp would save time if Edison decided to work on some other invention requiring a filament or anything analogous to a filament. For example, his long and costly labor testing carbonized cotton as a filament candidate significantly accelerated his later work on the carbon button transmitter, a great improvement on Alexander Graham Bell's telephone—indeed, so great an improvement that the carbon button transmitter was used in telephone handsets well into the 1970s.

Despite the demonstrated utility and longevity of the carbon button transmitter, some later commentators have denigrated the device as one of Edison's many "minor" inventions. In fact, it may not be proper to call it an invention at all, but rather an innovation or, even more accurately, a refinement of an invention (Bell's telephone). Considered as an innovation or a refinement, however, the carbon button transmitter is hardly minor, since it greatly increased the volume and fidelity—and therefore the usefulness—of telephone transmission. This improvement did not prove that Thomas Edison was a greater inventor than Alexander Graham Bell, but it did demonstrate Edison's broader and deeper knowledge of the properties of certain substances. Possessing this knowledge, Edison was able to focus it sharply on a specific problem with Bell's telephone transmitter, and, in doing so, he transformed the instrument from a clumsy—if astounding—device into an indispensable fixture of modern civilization.

Become a funnel for innovation. Begin with the widest possible knowledge of a subject area, then apply it—funnel it down—to the most sharply defined issue or problem. This typically requires front loading the creative process by "cutting and trying" a great many options. Time and labor invested at this front end save time and labor at the other end, when the options are applied to a specific problem or issue. This method also improves the odds of creating a genuine innovation, refinement, or improvement because it brings to bear the widest possible range of options to achieve the most sharply focused results.

Lesson 9: Know Properties, Not Theories

Edison was always more interested in the properties of substances— in which he saw the potential for practical, creative application— than in theories about how things worked. For example, when he discovered that compressed carbon was highly sensitive to variable electric currents, he created what became the carbon button transmitter, an innovation that greatly increased the sensitivity and the fidelity of telephone transmission.

The carbon button proved to be one of Edison's most profitable and enduring innovations, lasting (as noted) well into the 1970s. Yet, in classic Edison fashion, the inventor persisted in exploring the properties of compressed carbon even after he had successfully created and marketed his new transmitter. At normal operating temperatures, a carbon button amplified sound transmission, but, Edison discovered, when it was heated it distorted sound transmission. Because he was on the hunt for practical, profitable applications of the properties of substances, Edison could not have been blamed if he had paid little attention to this phenomenon. After all, what profit was there in distorting sound transmission?

None, as far as Edison knew at the time. Yet he nevertheless took careful note of this apparently useless property of the carbon button, carefully filed it away—for while he was willing to risk money, he was never willing to risk losing an idea or an observation—and in 1877 when the American astronomer Samuel Pierpont Langley asked him to design a supersensitive thermometer capable of quantifying the heat emitted by the sun's corona in a forthcoming total eclipse, his mind went back to the carbon button and its reaction to heat, which became the heart of an instrument he called the tasimeter.

It was a handheld device with a funnel—rather like the horn of an Edison phonograph—which focused heat on a piece of vulcanite, a specially manufactured kind of very hard rubber. Edison knew that a property of vulcanite was expansion with rising temperature. When the heat focused on the vulcanite increased, the hard rubber both compressed and heated up a carbon button positioned beneath it. In response to the temperature change, the button expanded against the compression, its electrical property of resistance changing with its change in size, however minute that change in size was. The change in resistance was read out on the dial of a battery-powered galvanometer, providing a quantification of the amount of heat reaching the carbon button.

With the tasimeter, Edison not only found a use for an apparently useless observed property of his carbon button, he also applied his customary process of invention by analogy in order to tease out that use.

The process of analogy worked like this: Whereas the carbon button had been developed to transmit shifts in sound waves, Edison saw an analogy between sound wave changes and changes in temperature. He was therefore able to adapt the carbon button to the analogous but very different application of transmitting shifts in temperature. Indeed, the tasimeter device was sufficiently sensitive to register a temperature change of 10^{-6} degrees Fahrenheit—highly remarkable for the time.

By thoroughly understanding the properties—the inherent potential—of whatever materials you work with (and this includes ideas and people as well as physical substances), you increase your chances of discovering new applications for all that you already possess or have access to. In this way, you maximize your creative assets, whatever they may be.

Lesson 10: Understand Hands-On: Touch Everything

As an innovative industrialist, Thomas Edison was eager to employ the most talented and best-educated workers he could find. But there was a problem. He diagnosed a crisis in American education, one (he claimed) that often deprived him—and others—of the very best workers. The problem was not a deficiency in the American intellect or an intellectual weakness in the "younger generation," but a defect in the American system of education, which Edison derided as a "relic of past ages," consisting of "parrot-like repetitions," the "dull study of twenty-six hieroglyphs." In a diary entry from January 4, 1914, the inventor complained that "the young of the present" were being condemned to study "groups of hieroglyphs"—the innumerable words on the pages of innumerable books.

Here is an object. I place it in the hands of a child. I tell him to look at it. If we begin before we have hardened and dried his mind he studies the object with kindling enthusiasm. The mind of the child is naturally active. Why should we make him take his impressions of things through the ear when he may be able to see? . . . One glance, if he sees the thing itself, is better than two hours of studying about a thing, which he does not see.

Edison proclaimed himself an enthusiastic advocate of the progressive Montessori method of education because it "teaches through play" and, in so doing, follows the "natural instincts of the human being." Posing the question of what system of education would better succeed in America, Edison suggested introducing one that "shows to those who learn the actual thing—not the ghost of it," the mere shell of reality that is buried in the words on the pages of so many books.

Book learning at the expense of unmediated exposure to reality "casts the brain into a mould," Edison believed, discouraging original thought, compelling the passive acceptance of received wisdom, and thereby fostering conservatism as well as breeding fear, from which, the inventor declared, "comes ignorance."

> What we call conservatism is largely a result of a hard and fast way of teaching, a worship of the twenty-six hieroglyphs, the adoration of symbols, which fosters the creed that nothing can be done which has not been done by our fathers.

Contrary to popular Edison lore, the largely self-taught inventor had no prejudice against college-educated men; he enthusiastically hired many of them. But he did believe that the "present-day college graduate" had little practical understanding of the real world, mainly because he tended to object to work, "especially if it is dirty."

Would you be educated in the real world? Get dirty, Edison advised. Touch, shape, take apart, and put together the innumerable devices on which modern civilization is built. Work with the things themselves, not their pale shadows as traced in theory and abstract discussion.

For Edison, innovation was never theoretical. It was always hands-on. The first step toward creative, profitable innovation (as Edison saw it) was to grasp the realities of the environment in which you proposed to innovate. After seeing and feeling these firsthand, the next step was to determine what new shapes these realities might be made to take in order to make them more useful, efficient, and profitable. For Edison there was no alternative: Innovation always required dirty hands.

Lesson 11: Miss No Detail

On July 12, 1885, Thomas Edison recorded in his diary: "I think freckles on the skin are due to some salt of Iron, sunlight brings them out by reducing them from high to low state of oxidation—perhaps with a powerful magnet applied for some time, and then with proper chemicals, these mud holes of beauty might be removed."

It is an odd, apparently random observation from the "Wizard of Menlo Park." It comes in the diary apropos of nothing—and that is just the point. Edison was a compulsive observer; he harnessed his natural inclination by making it a deliberate, conscious practice to miss no detail in all that he observed and, having noted a detail, to make a written or drawn record of it. To be sure, there is a strong element of free association in his observation on freckles, yet Edison almost never allowed free association to remain absolutely free. No sooner did the idea occur to him that freckles might be due to the action of sunlight on a ferrous substance in the skin than he tied down this apparently random and unbidden observation to a hint of a possibly useful—that is, practical and profitable—application. If there is a ferrous substance at work, he reasoned, perhaps the combination of a magnet and "proper chemicals" might be used to pull it out, thus removing freckles.

Acquire the habit of seeing the world actively instead of passively. Look at reality for how you might shape, adapt, and change it in order to solve problems and produce profit. Freckles, like electricity, are properties of the environment. Edison was just as willing to engage with freckles as he was with electricity.

Lesson 12: Know What's Going On Inside

Edison is often both praised and condemned as a trial-and-error inventor, a man who knew how to create not by system and theory but by the blunt dint of main strength and seemingly limitless endurance. This picture has an element of truth, just as there is some truth in the view of Edison as first and foremost a practical journeyman who disdained theory and theoretical knowledge. Yet neither of these views tells the whole truth about the Edison method.

Without doubt, Edison's approach to invention and innovation was hands-on. Characteristically, he began by identifying a problem or a need, then he sketched a means of addressing it. This conceptual phase completed, he would set about overseeing the transformation of his sketches into an actual experimental prototype. That this process typically went forward with little or no theoretical prelude did not mean that Edison was uninterested in understanding just how and why his inventions worked. His method of testing his prototypes always included intense observation over an extended period. Edison never regarded what he made as just so many black boxes, devices that either worked or failed to work, that either sold or failed to sell. Always, he peered inside and strove to understand precisely what was going on. The knowledge he gained from these testing observations was rarely reduced to theory. Instead, the inventor took careful note of the working properties of a device and all of its components. Whereas for the so-called pure scientist, fundamental knowledge is theoretical knowledge, for Edison it was first and foremost working knowledge—yet still fundamental knowledge: an understanding of inherent properties with an eye toward manipulating them to produce devices of ever greater utility, efficiency, economy, and simplicity.

Trial and error can be a powerful, if awfully blunt, creative tool, but it is no substitute for discovering how things work so that they can be made to work better. For the inventor and innovator, this is what constitutes fundamental knowledge.

3

HOW TO USE EVERYTHING

Lesson 13: Profit from Disability

Edison, the man who invented—among many other things—the phonograph and an improved system of telephone transmission, was hard of hearing and sometimes even referred to himself as deaf. Indeed, his hearing steadily deteriorated over the course of his life, so that, near its end, his condition did approach total deafness.

Most authorities believe that his hearing loss was the result of an early bout with scarlet fever and a childhood history of colds and other upper respiratory disorders, which led to fluid retention in the middle ear. Popular mythology—partly created by Edison himself—ascribes his hearing problems to a drubbing he took at the hands of Alexander Stevenson, conductor on the Grand Trunk Western Railway. One day, while Edison was working as a news butcher in his early teens, an experiment went very wrong in the corner of the baggage car where he used to print his newspaper and pursue his researches; chemicals burst into flame, and the interior of the car started burning. Working frantically, Edison and Stevenson were able to contain and extinguish the blaze, but once the fire was safely out, the conductor turned his wrath on the young experimenter, unceremoniously tossing his equipment out of the train when it stopped at Smith's Creek—and for good measure boxing Edison's ears before sending him out the door as well.

That is one story. Another tale—also sometimes told by Edison himself—has Stevenson using the boy's ears to pull him up into the baggage car. One day, just as the train was getting into motion,

Edison, burdened with a load of newspapers, had no hand free to hoist himself into the moving car. Stevenson used his ears as convenient handles, but (the mature Edison reported) "something snapped" inside his head, and his hearing deteriorated thereafter.

Whatever the cause of his hearing loss—whether common childhood disease or semi-mythical boyhood hard knocks—Edison was not to be pitied for his disability. "Broadway," he blithely proclaimed, "is as quiet to me as a country village is to a person with normal hearing," and, as a result, nothing could distract him from the mental labor of invention. Edison seemed genuinely to regard his semi-deafness as a gift of nature, which spared him from all manner of time-wasting distraction, ranging from parties and social gatherings to the incessant din of the very industrial revolution of which he was so much a part. Like that other celebrated hearing-impaired creator, Ludwig van Beethoven, deafness gave Edison a claim on a private world of the most sublime exclusivity, one that turned him inward, facilitating the discovery of his own imagination.

> Disability? Asset? Exploit whoever you are and whatever you have to give your creative work an individual stamp and the freshness of unique inspiration.

Lesson 14: Lose No Idea

As a young telegrapher beginning to dabble in invention, Thomas Edison made it a habit to carry a pocket notebook in which he jotted or drew up ideas as they occurred to him. He was determined to capture the stream of notions that passed through his mind—and to capture them the very moment they passed. Edison had a prodigious memory, and he believed that a well-developed memory was the most important asset any creative person could possess. Nevertheless, he was clearly unwilling to rely on memory alone. He made notes wherever he went and whenever an idea came to light for him. In his middle age, after he set up a laboratory-workshop in New Jersey and then, later, in Fort Myers, Florida, he placed notebooks on almost every horizontal surface throughout his shop, admonishing all his workers and researchers to write down or draw up any ideas they had and to do so whenever they had them. Nobody was going to lose an idea on his watch.

"Genius," Edison famously declared, "is 1 percent inspiration and 99 percent perspiration," but he was never willing to give up that 1 percent. It is folly to wait passively for inspiration, but it is even more foolish—tragic, in fact—to lose inspiration when it finally does come. Capture all ideas. Do so without censorship or judgment. Get them down. Evaluate them later. Sacrifice nothing. Discard nothing.

Lesson 15: Be Exhaustive

Who has not heard Edison's most-often quoted maxim, the one about inspiration and perspiration just mentioned in Lesson 14?

The process by which Thomas Edison invented and innovated was characteristically exhaustive, productive indeed of much sweat. The most familiar case in point was the inventor's worldwide search for the ideal filament material to use in his incandescent lamp. He commissioned the collection and testing of thousands of substances, eliminating those that failed just as enthusiastically as he selected those that showed promise. For Edison, any trial, any experiment that yielded data was a success, even if it did not produce the result that had been anticipated or hoped for.

The exhaustive approach was a hallmark of Edison's creative career. In his early work on duplex telegraphy (a telegraphic system that allowed for two signals to be sent simultaneously on the same wire in opposite directions) and diplex telegraphy (which simultaneously sent two messages in the same direction on a single line), Edison created and tested over a brief period no fewer than twenty-three different and complete systems. He reported that "nine were failures, four practical successes, and ten were all right; one or two worked rather bad, but the principle was good, and if they were to be used could be improved in detail; eight were good."

What is especially interesting here is that Edison refused to see the results in terms of black and white, failure or success. The different approaches succeeded or failed in varying degrees, and his evaluations reflected that reality. Moreover, while it might seem natural to pursue one or more of the eight devices that proved to be "good," he seems to have been particularly intrigued by the one or two that "worked rather bad," because they nevertheless embodied a sound principle, which, with further refinement, might prove highly useful. This was no process of mere trial and error. It was trial and evaluation, the acquisition of knowledge.

It is as destructive to seize impulsively on your first success as it is to become discouraged by your first failure. Whether successful or not, try again—and again, and yet again, until you have exhausted all feasible and significant alternatives. Success and failure are rarely binary. Performance is typically a continuum, a matter of degree, balance, and compromise. Capture reality faithfully by observing and evaluating all results in all degrees.

Lesson 16: Appreciate Your Ignorance

Just as he made use of success as well as failure—the first provided data on what worked, the second yielded equally valuable information on what did not work—Edison found that knowledge and ignorance were of comparable if not equal value. Whereas knowledge pointed the direction in any given research project or experiment, saving time and effort by allowing the experimenter to focus only on the most likely approaches, ignorance opened the mind by obliging the ignorant experimenter to try every conceivable approach. To be sure, this was labor-intensive and time-consuming, but it also multiplied the possibilities of making new, unexpected discoveries.

Ignorance both invited and necessitated pure empiricism—the exhaustive observation, cut-and-try, trial-and-error methodology most often associated with Thomas Edison. In practice, however, the inventor rarely employed a purely empirical approach. More usually, he modified empiricism by drawing on his own experience and expertise as well as that of his growing staff of scientists and mechanics. Moreover, a preliminary step in any major Edison research project was an intensive survey of the existing literature in the field. At his most creative, Edison managed to strike a balance between knowledge and ignorance, never relinquishing empiricism but nevertheless focusing it—albeit not so narrowly as to become blind to the unexpected.

> Ignorance opens the way for discovery. For the inventor–innovator, the purpose of knowledge is to accelerate the empiricism that is born of pure ignorance.

Lesson 17: Sharpen Your Tools

Popular mythology paints the youthful Thomas Edison as a telegrapher of almost supernatural skill. In fact, he never rose above the status of journeyman among fellow telegraphers. Although he always denied it, he was certainly hampered by his bad hearing, and if he hoped he could compensate for his shortcomings as a receiver by becoming a great sender, he was doomed to disappointment. Many men were faster at the key than he was.

Edison coped with his deficiencies through technology, but also by developing a unique personal skill. The latter approach is especially interesting because it illustrates the inventor's habit of viewing entire processes whenever he was looking for a path to innovation. He tried, at least in the initial conceptual stages of invention, to avoid focusing exclusively on segments of any given process.

Here is how this worked in the case of Edison's bad hearing. About the physical disability itself, Edison could do nothing. About the speed of his telegraphic transmission—his mastery of the key— he did as much as he could, but that, as it turned out, fell rather short of what the most adept senders could do. As most telegraphers would have seen it, the only way for Edison to have improved his performance would have been to practice, practice, practice in order to gain speed. Edison, however, believed that he was already transmitting as fast as he ever could, and so he looked forward a step further in the process.

Telegraphy is about sending and receiving, but, in the 1800s, it was also about transcribing—writing down messages in a form that nontelegraphers could read. This was not exactly an aspect of the technology of telegraphy, but it was undeniably a part of the process. Edison looked to it and developed a handwriting style that was small, fast, and acutely legible—so legible that at least one contemporary described it as "plain as print." The result was that, while many telegraphers transmitted and received faster than Edison, very few could complete the entire telegraphic process with greater speed and accuracy. Their transcriptions were slower and sloppier—less legible. Edison therefore emerged as a master telegrapher, despite his significant weaknesses.

Did Thomas Edison have the good fortune to have been born a great calligrapher? No, not according to him. He developed his unique handwriting through many hours of experimenting with his natural penmanship in an effort to find or create a style that enabled maximum speed without sacrificing legibility. Reducing the size of the characters was part of this. Making shorter strokes took less time than making longer ones. He also prepared himself mentally for speed. His journeyman skills were more than sufficient to receive and transcribe ordinary messages. Press copy, however, was far more demanding. Edison decided to prepare his mind for efficiently and accurately receiving such copy by devouring two or three newspapers a day in order to stock his imagination with the current news. Thus immersed in current events, he was able to transcribe press copy accurately even when he was not fast enough to write down the messages word for word. His prepared imagination supplied all the missing material.

> First: Make the very best of what you have. If others have better tools, then ensure that the ones you do have are extra sharp. Next: Avoid tripping over any step in a process. Compensate for a stumble at point B with a bold leap at point D. It's the end result that counts.

Lesson 18: Embrace Problems

Edison welcomed failure. He embraced it. He was rarely able to predict everything that would go wrong with a design he had sketched until that design had been prototyped by his machinists and shop men and had, in some way or other, come up short. As he made the rounds of his shop floor, his men would tell him what had gone wrong, and Edison would immediately set about searching for solutions.

The inventor extended his embrace of problems to products that had already been marketed and sold. He always carefully analyzed customer complaints and used them as the basis for incremental improvements. These innovations on the original inventions were often in themselves patentable, and thus Thomas Edison racked up his world-record number of U.S. patents.

> Problems drive innovation. Embrace them and be driven.

Lesson 19: Problems Are Directions

When Edison decided to reinvent the storage battery, his very first step was to inventory the problems of the batteries already on the market. They were legion. Early storage batteries were nasty and unreliable contraptions. They lost their capacity to hold a charge after repeated discharge and recharge cycles. They contained solid lead electrodes, which were very heavy—a great disadvantage when the batteries were used to power electric vehicles. In Edison's day, it was more expensive to run a car on electricity derived from storage batteries than to run a car on gasoline. Moreover, because the batteries were so heavy, an electric car had to be built on a sturdier chassis than the gasoline-powered equivalent, something that raised the cost of electric vehicles. Thus, these vehicles were not only more expensive to run than gasoline-fueled cars, they were also costlier to purchase in the first place.

Added to problems of reliability and weight was the fact that storage batteries required frequent charging—a process that had to be carried out with great care. Battery electrolytes had to be replenished frequently. Moreover, the electrolytes, a sulfuric acid solution, were dangerous.

Where others might regard this menu of problems as daunting, a reason to avoid getting into the storage battery business, Edison saw it as a veritable inventory of opportunities. The list of problems was a list of assignments, a manual of directions for building a better battery. Reviewing the list, he instantly knew that his improved battery would need to have a substantial storage capacity relative to its weight, that it would have to be as nearly maintenance free as possible, that it would need to resist deterioration with each charge and recharge cycle, that it would need to be capable of rapid recharging, and that it would have to withstand rough treatment—without presenting the dangers of sulfuric acid. Problems? What Edison had was a list of desired specifications: a leg up on innovation. Thus focused and guided, he went to work.

Each feature an existing device lacks and each job it fails to perform adequately are precise prescriptions for innovation. Every unsolved problem is an opportunity.

Lesson 20: The Limits of the Problem Approach

Edison welcomed problems because he understood that a problem always contains the seed of its own solution. As he saw it, each problem identified an unsatisfied need or set of needs and thereby prodded the inventor into creating a solution.

Case in point: In 1887, when Edison saw a demonstration of Alexander Graham Bell's version of the phonograph, the graphophone, he noted that Bell had solved several problems relating to the clarity of reproduced sound, but had introduced a new problem caused by the soft wax, called ozokerite, with which he coated his recording cylinders. Although an ozokerite recording was very clear on first playing, the recording surface quickly became dulled and the sound reproduction degraded with repeated playing. In addition to rapidly wearing down, the soft wax tended to clog the reproducing stylus.

As usual, Edison greeted the problem as an opening for an innovation. He focused, logically enough, on finding a better recording medium, a substance that would retain the benefits of clarity and fidelity afforded by the ozokerite, but that would be far more durable. By means of a series of experiments, he found that paraffin mixed with resin yielded a sensitive yet durable recording surface, and he set his assistants to work testing various combinations and formulas.

That was all well and good. But even as he put his men to work in the chemical lab, he himself took an entirely different direction, sketching out a "receiving needle [that] never touches the surface of the record but is itself electrified and . . . attracted to the surface more or less as the record is indented."

It was an extraordinary idea. Edison had conceived nothing less than a kind of magnetic pickup or playback head, which could be called a hybrid of mechanical and electromagnetic recording technologies, except for the fact that the electromagnetic technology (namely the tape recorder) did not yet exist. The potential of Edison's novel conception was great. Intensively pursued, the electromagnetic pickup might have been the heart of a recording and playback system more sensitive and accurate than anything yet in existence. Moreover, because the "needle" did not physically contact the record, wear and tear would be reduced to zero, and records would have been virtually permanent.

But Edison never pursued this radical technology—not because he considered it unworkable, but because his experimenters succeeded in solving the soft wax problem chemically. Their direct solution was a marketable *innovation*, which, for Edison, was sufficient to preclude the necessity for a radically new *invention*. This was by no means a failure or false step. The new cylinders were an improvement and therefore made money for Edison. Yet settling for innovation in this case did abruptly end work in a novel field of invention with far more exciting potential. In this case, Edison sacrificed embarking on the development of an entirely new technology in favor of tinkering—albeit productively—with one that was already familiar, that required far less labor to invent, and that did not render his own existing technology—the Edison phonograph—obsolete.

> Problem solving is a powerful driver of innovation. The question remains: Should you stop when the problem is solved? Innovation is usually cheaper and more expedient than full-blown invention. But what if the price of innovation is the end of invention?

Lesson 21: Use Disaster

"Edison's folly," it was called—a decade-long endeavor to create an industrial plant to electromagnetically separate iron from very low-grade ore. Had he succeeded in making it work on a consistently commercial level, Edison would have become the nation's source of cheap iron and steel. He would have created yet another civilization-altering invention. But he never was able to make the process work reliably on a full commercial scale, and the venture stretched on as a time- and cash-consuming disaster.

Yet Thomas Edison was determined to find a use even for disaster. Deciding to get in on the business of Portland cement, he was determined to recoup as much of his iron ore processing investment as possible by using or adapting his equipment, especially his advanced ore-crushing machinery, for manufacturing artificial cement. To a remarkable degree, Edison succeeded in recycling his physical plant, but he did not allow his strong desire to make good his losses overshadow his instincts as an innovator. Where he could reuse or modify existing equipment, he did so—and eagerly—but where he saw the need for an entirely new invention, he set about working on it with even more brio.

A key step in the manufacture of Portland cement was "roasting" the ground-up blend of cement rock and limestone to produce what the industry called "clinker." Edison already had the most advanced crushing technology available—he had developed it for his ill-fated ore-separating plant—and he had determined that his ability to produce a finer grind than any other cement maker would yield a superior product. In Edison's day, accepted Portland cement industry practice called for roasting the ground material in 60-foot rotary kilns. Edison could have purchased these for his plant, but, after carefully analyzing the manufacturing process, he had identified a weakness—and that opened the door to innovation. He wanted to build a much larger kiln, which would not only be more efficient than the industry standard, but would produce a much greater yield. Instead of a 60-foot kiln, he intended to build a 150-foot device to be fed by a pair of innovative high-pressure "coal guns" that would mix fuel and air in the kiln, creating a larger and more even roasting area within the vast rotary oven.

Edison knew that the major problem he would face with his giant kiln was building reliable machinery to rotate it, but he was also aware that there might be other problems, and so he began the invention process by modeling a single section of the kiln in wood to study it in three dimensions. This led him to innovate even more ambitiously by designing as much of the machinery as possible to run completely automatically, thereby reducing the need for paid employees. By the time he was finished, Edison had not only salvaged a good bit of the investment that otherwise would have been lost on his disastrous iron-extraction venture, he used this resurrection to innovate and invent vastly improved methods of making Portland cement.

> *Waste not*, the proverb runs. But let salvage be an inspiration and a new beginning, not an end in itself. Reuse the past, but do not become locked into it.

Lesson 22: "No Experiments Are Useless"

Early in his inventing career, Edison made extensive use of a new class of venture capitalists, men of business who were willing to invest, not in going concerns or even in start-up companies, but in experimental research itself. Nevertheless, even among this willing group of financial pioneers, Edison often found himself having to defend the work in which they had invested. To one venture capitalist he endeavored to explain the poor performance of a perforator for an automatic telegraph system he was working on as something of "no consequence," because "it was an experiment as I told you before, not made to show but to Satisfy me that I was all right." When this same investor carped that some of the experiments he had financed were "useless," Edison replied that, once the investor had "more experience in this business [of inventing], he [would] find that *No experiments are useless*."

Edison understood that what others labeled as "failed experiments"—experiments that did not produce positive, immediately tangible results—almost always yielded important data. The best failures produced an abundance of data, and, at the very least, a failed experiment eliminated whatever approach to a problem was under consideration and thereby made way for some alternative. Whatever had lessons to teach was useful, even if not immediately profitable.

> No experiment that produces data—insight—can be called useless. So-called failures should be analyzed as closely as positive successes.

Lesson 23: Fertile Failure

Edison's proudest boast was that he never allowed himself "to become discouraged under any circumstances." After conducting "thousands of experiments on a certain project without solving the problem," one of the inventor's associates "expressed discouragement and disgust over our having failed 'to find out anything.'" Edison responded to the disgruntled experimenter by "cheerily" assuring him "that we *had* learned something . . . [the] certainty that the thing couldn't be done that way, and that we would have to try some other way."

Edison was interested in the results of his experiments. It almost did not matter whether or not a given result was successful—that is, immediately useful or immediately profitable. Whether positive or negative, an experimental result was a *result:* data, knowledge, fact. He believed that we "sometimes learn a lot from our failures," although he added an intriguing qualifier: "if we have put into the effort the best thought and work we are capable of."

That clause is crucial to the creative exploitation of failure. A haphazard experiment that nevertheless results in a useful product can be counted a profitable success. The annals of science and technology are full of so-called happy accidents. In contrast, the haphazard, careless, sloppy, half-hearted experiment that results in failure has no value whatsoever, because it is impossible to know whether the failure was the result of faulty experimental technique or of an idea, principle, or concept that simply will not work. Only if the failure is the result of a careful process—the "best thought and work we are capable of"—can one reasonably assess the reason for the failure and thereby learn something of value. To be able to declare definitively that *Method A does not work* represents significant research progress, whereas to conclude that *the experiment failed for some reason or other* is not progress at all.

> All experiments sincerely conceived and meticulously carried out are by their nature "successful." The only outright failure is a failure of absolute commitment.

Lesson 24: Make Defects Their Own Remedy

As a telegrapher, Edison achieved competence rather than mastery. He became a journeyman, not a genius, of the code key. Yet he was never content with confinement to journeyman work. For telegraphers in the 1860s and 1870s, receiving and transcribing long, complex newspaper stories was work reserved for the true masters, experts who had achieved consistent speed and accuracy.

Edison found it very hard to keep pace with these messages, but instead of despairing, he found in his weakness a source of strength, a spur to innovation. As noted in Lesson 17, one avenue of innovation Edison pursued was nontechnical. He developed a unique style of small, fast, highly legible handwriting. In addition to this solution, he pursued a technological innovation. He obtained a pair of Morse code registers and used one of these to record the incoming message—the dots and dashes—as indentations on a strip of paper; the second one he used as a playback device, running the strip embossed by the first register through the second one, but at a slower pace than the standard forty words per minute. This allowed him to transcribe a perfect copy of each message every time. (Of ultimately even greater importance, the innovation started him thinking about the possibilities of recording sound and set him on the path to inventing the phonograph.)

Edison's solution to his problem with high-speed telegraph transcription was a genuine technological innovation—not an invention. That is, he did not invent a new device, he used existing devices in a new way—not merely to record telegraphic messages but to play them back, and not just to play them back but to do so at a speed that compensated for human weakness. Actually, the Edison innovation did more than merely compensate. By allowing him to create virtually perfect transcriptions, it improved on the work that even the best telegraphers could turn out.

It was typical of Edison to profit from defects or to make defects compensate for the very problems they caused. This happened when he was working on a quadruplex telegraph system, which would allow four messages to be transmitted simultaneously over a single line. Edison discovered that the process of repeatedly reversing current (necessary for the quadruplex to work) caused a relay to lose its magnetism at a critical moment, thereby producing a garbled signal. After experimenting, Edison was unable to find any way to prevent the loss of magnetism, so he decided to create a workaround, which he called a "bug trap." He gave up trying to *prevent* the relay from releasing at the critical moment and instead devised a means of using that release to energize another relay, which closed the circuit the other failed to close and thereby compensated for the loss of magnetism. In this way, the defect—the loss of magnetism on one relay—triggered another relay, which compensated for the failure.

> Defects, flaws, weaknesses—all are fertile ground for innovation. Don't hide them. Uncover them. Use them. Build on them. Convert them into strengths.

4

INVESTING

Lesson 25: The Ideal Executive

By the second decade of the twentieth century, Edison had formulated a questionnaire for all who sought employment in his laboratories, workshops, or the executive level of his manufacturing companies. Educators and others of the era regarded the questionnaire as quirky, even perverse. And no wonder. It consisted of an almost random series of questions, such as *What is the capital of Nevada? Where is the world's primary source of mahogany? In what country is Timbuctoo? Who was Desmoulins? Who was Kit Carson? Who was Blaise Pascal?*

Perhaps the oddest of all the features of this questionnaire was that Edison really had no interest in whether or not a particular applicant knew any of the things he asked them. All he wanted to assess was the quality of a prospective employee's memory, and the only method he knew for doing this was to ask for random facts and see how many an applicant recalled and how many he had forgotten—for Edison assumed that any reasonably well-educated person would have been exposed, at some time or other, to the information he asked about.

Thomas Edison placed a high premium on a keen, well-stocked, and facile memory. To the question, *What is the most important qualification for an executive?* he believed there was a very simple answer. The most important qualification was a fine memory.

It was a matter of efficiency. He explained that whenever he called on one of his executives for a decision, he wanted it immediately. When the members of that executive's department wanted a decision, they also wanted it right away. The executive most likely to render a rapid decision—and a well-informed one—was the executive possessed of the most ready knowledge, the person whose memory was stocked with useful facts.

As Edison stocked his laboratories and workshops with virtually every conceivable substance, so he wanted his mind and those of his top employees stocked with virtually every conceivable fact that might be of any use in the process of invention, manufacture, or marketing. Whatever else an innovator was, for Edison he was a person whose mind was stocked with the known. Thus furnished, it was a mind prepared to venture into what was not yet known and to create what had not yet been created.

> Possessing a fine creative imagination—whatever that may be—is doubtless valuable for any inventor or innovator, but it is at least equally certain that the more you know about your field and the fields related to yours the better your chances of creating and selling useful and successful products and processes and the better your chances of creating and selling them with the greatest efficiency and the least expenditure of time and cash.

Lesson 26: Insure the Permanency of an Investment

Edison held that there was a "law in commercial things as in nature." He believed that if you attempted to "obtain more profit than the general average," you would be "immediately punished by competition." He therefore adopted a practice of "insuring the permanency of an investment" by lowering prices on his products sufficiently to remove any "inducement to others to come in and ruin" the market. That is, he strove to position himself so that no one could make what he made cheaper. Through a combination of advanced manufacturing and a willingness to reduce profit margin, Edison's early electric lamps were so inexpensive that he hoped "to make it positively impossible for [competition] to exist." Having created a market, Edison sought to maintain control of it.

Figure into the innovation equation the role of competition. Can you, like Edison, formulate ways to manage the market you propose to enter?

Lesson 27: Invest in Assets

Why does winning the lottery so often fail to make the winner happy? One reason is the failure to turn newfound riches into wealth. Lottery winners often rush out to buy things—cars, houses, furniture, vacations, and the like—that constitute expenses rather than assets, riches rather than wealth. When Edison sold a quadruplex telegraph system to the financier Jay Gould in 1875, he immediately invested the cash proceeds from the sale in books and scientific equipment for his laboratory. He plowed his profits back into his enterprise. It was an investment in assets—really, in his biggest asset: himself.

Create wealth rather than riches by investing in assets, which will build your enterprise by enhancing your ability to innovate.

Lesson 28: Start Small, Scale Up

The phrase "trial and error" is often applied—and applied indiscriminately, almost automatically—to the creative method of Thomas Edison. Where some projects were concerned, this description was accurate enough, as when Edison searched far

and wide for the perfect material to use as an electric light filament. Theory could not answer the question of what material
would work best. No one had any experience passing electrical
current through materials for the purpose of creating light. The
only option in surveying this utterly unexplored territory was to
acquire a thorough understanding of the properties of a very wide
range of materials under current and in a vacuum. The only way
to gain this understanding was to observe each of these materials
under precisely those conditions. The method, therefore, was trial,
error, and close observation.

But when Edison tackled projects that were not well suited to
the trial, error, observation approach, he found other ways. For
instance, with projects that required building on a large scale—
constructing massive machinery or entire processing plants—trial
and error was far too expensive a method for developing innovation. Instead, Edison turned to modeling, experimenting with
processes and manufacturing techniques on a small scale before
embarking on the full-size real thing.

Edison found that scale modeling was by no means a perfect
experimental method. First, there was the time and expense of
building a model, introducing between the experimental and
production phases of a project an intermediate phase. More important was the fact that many physical processes cannot be accurately
scaled down. One can build small-scale equipment and machinery
of course, but there is no guarantee that it will behave in miniature
the same way it would behave at full size.

In an important respect, modeling was for Edison a compromise
with reality intended to avoid the high price tag reality sometimes
presents, including the potentially catastrophic expense of failure.
For Edison, however, modeling was more than a mere compromise.
The inventor–innovator habitually worked out solutions to problems
visually, by making sketches. For relatively simple processes, a sketch
was sufficient for him to understand the relation of one mechanical
component to another. Likewise, sketches were sometimes valuable
for visualizing certain electric and electrochemical processes. But

when entire systems were under consideration, massive in scale and complex in operation, modeling was a necessary three-dimensional step beyond the two-dimensional sketch. It was not just an attempt to try out a process, it was a means of visualizing it, imagining it, and perfecting it, and was therefore an essential step in the actual course of invention.

> Modeling can serve both as a proof-of-concept step, taken before committing major resources to a full-size project prototype, and as a multi-dimensional means of continuing the process of invention. A model can serve as both a small-scale prototype, with limited cost and relatively low risk, and as a conceptual platform, inviting and enabling creative risks that would be impractical at full scale.

Lesson 29: Build an Invention Factory

When Edison established his laboratory–workshop complex at Menlo Park, New Jersey, in the 1870s, his objective was to rationalize and regularize the process of invention, to take it out of the realm of hit-or-miss inspiration and luck, and to create what he called an "invention factory." The industrial revolution had already passed into its first great maturity. Mass production of all sorts of goods was a well-established fact. What Edison now perceived was that invention itself—hitherto regarded as the product of more or less whimsical inventive "genius"—could be incorporated into the industrial mass-production process.

Menlo Park, the invention factory, was itself a great invention, but, like most everything else Edison created, it was by no means a radical departure from existing practices, sui generis, without precedent. In fact, Menlo Park was built firmly on tradition. Its practices, its very atmosphere harked back to an epoch preceding industrial mass production—the age and culture of individual craftsmanship. The laboratory–workshops at Menlo Park had some of the features of modern factories, but they were staffed more by a collection of individual craftsmen than by modern industrial workers. At the same time, it is also true that the Menlo Park facility elevated the craft tradition and culture to a new order of magnitude, a new—industrial—scale. It was this elevation and expansion that constituted the true innovation.

For Edison, the measure of Menlo Park's success as an invention *factory* was its reliability and speed. He was determined to produce "a minor invention every ten days and a big thing every six months or so." Over his working lifetime of some sixty-one years, Edison actually averaged eighteen patents annually, or one patent every twenty days—not very far from the goal he had set at the outset of the Menlo Park years.

Edison approached innovation as itself an innovation. In part, it was a bold rethinking of the traditional concept of inventive inspiration, which was typically regarded as the product of unpredictable genius. In part also, the Menlo Park facility was a conservative return to the pre-industrial culture of individual craftsmanship. Finally, and also in part, it was a thoroughgoing engagement with contemporary industrial mass-production methods. In short, Edison used every means at his disposal to render invention as reliable and as regular as possible, thereby ensuring a stable economic basis for ongoing experiments, which might or might not produce directly profitable results.

Lesson 30: Support the Shop

Surveying the career of Thomas Edison, the obvious thing to do is marvel at the range of his invention: telegraphy, telephony, the phonograph, motion picture technology, incandescent electric lighting, power generation, battery technology, ore processing, cement production, rubber production, and so on.

The big things, the civilization-altering inventions, these are the obvious Edison projects. Less obvious are the many instances in which the inventor carved out sometimes arcane specialties and innovated within them. Although his range was undeniably and remarkably broad, the vast majority of his thousand-plus patents were for variations on devices in a limited number of areas, especially telegraphic communications.

Edison never wanted to be tied down to a particular field. His drive to innovate and invent was restless. Nevertheless, he realized that this restless urge and imperative for creative liberty had to be supported financially, and so, to support his shop, he dedicated a certain proportion of his inventive work to creating reliable income streams. Instead, therefore, of giving absolutely free rein to his imagination, he frequently turned to what was most familiar to him, the telegraph industry, and produced a steady flow of innovations that would (he was confident) produce a steady if unspectacular flow of revenue.

> Be seduced neither by the freedom of novelty nor by the apparent security of a creative rut. Balance the unknown with the known. By all means indulge your creativity, but also sustain rather than starve it. Do what you must to support your shop, then get on with the work of innovation.

Lesson 31: Build on the Weakest Points

Like most everyone else in his world, Thomas Edison was deeply impressed by what Alexander Graham Bell had achieved in 1876 with the telephone. This said, he was not overawed by the invention. A telephone had been invented, but *the* telephone had yet to be perfected. Instead of discouraging Edison from entering this field, Bell's breakthrough prompted him to begin his own experiments with what was widely called at the time the "talking telegraph." The fact was that Edison, this great inventor and innovator, a man who looked at the world a little differently from everyone else, had a hard time resisting the impulse to hop on an inviting bandwagon, especially when it was just getting under way.

Edison's chief approach to innovation was to build on existing or emerging technology by first identifying the weakest points in that technology and then planning how he would create improvements on them. The weaker the point he could identify, the greater the improvement he could make. Edison believed it was in the gulf yawning between original weakness and strong innovation that the possibility of introducing a compelling "must-have" commercial product lay.

As Edison saw it, the weakest point in the Bell telephone was the transmitter. Edison therefore immediately directed all of his telephone research toward improving this component. In Bell's transmitter, sound waves hit a diaphragm that vibrated a permanent magnet, which in turn induced a current in an electromagnet, thereby creating a continuous variable (or "undulating") current, which was transmitted along telephone lines to a receiver, which reversed the acoustic-electrical transformation process and thereby produced sound waves.

Bell's transmitter had two major weaknesses. The first was that the currents involved were so weak that they could be transmitted only over relatively short distances. The second was that transmission quality was poor, resulting in low-fidelity voice reproduction. Edison addressed the weak current issue by employing stronger battery current along the lines and using sound waves not to generate the current but to vary the strength of the current supplied by the batteries. By using a weak current to regulate a strong one, he significantly increased the range of telephone communication. As for the issue of fidelity, Edison addressed this by improving the diaphragm, at first linking the vibrating diaphragm to a contact that was pushed in and out of a liquid conductor, but soon turning to carbon in the form of a "button" fashioned out of so-called plumbago (black lead, or graphite). As usual, Edison and his men made hundreds of experiments with plumbago, pressing it into various shapes and combining it with many other substances in an effort to find a means of more efficiently and accurately transforming the sonically induced vibrations of the transmitter diaphragm into electrical signals. Ultimately, Edison created the carbon button transmitter, which was such an improvement that it came to dominate telephone transmitter technology for most of a century. Edison elevated Bell's breakthrough from the status of promising prototype to a full commercial product.

> In weakness there is strength. The weak points of any technology are neither to be regretted nor avoided, but rather probed and exploited. Weakness is what prepares the way for innovation. It is to the inventor what vacant land is to the builder. It is possibility. It is potential. It is promise.

Lesson 32: Become a Collector

Edison the inventor and industrialist regarded himself as first and foremost a collector. He collected ideas, he collected patents, he collected breakthroughs, he collected failures, he collected promising craftsmen, scientists, workers, and assistants, he collected equipment, and—as he pointed out when he contemplated building a new laboratory–workshop in West Orange, New Jersey, he collected "almost every conceivable material of every size." He reasoned that to invent and to manufacture with maximum productivity and at top speed an inventor had to have on hand as much as he could of what any conceivable project could possibly require. Such an inventory, he declared, would enable "a man [to] produce 10 times as much" as someone working in an ordinary laboratory setting could. An "experimenter," he wrote, "never knows 5 minutes ahead what he does want." Creative momentum, Edison believed, was a most precious commodity. To avoid squandering it by having to pause while some rare substance was located, Edison actually planned to obtain "a quantity of every known substance on the face of the globe." If he could thoroughly stock his shop, he felt confident that he would be master of what was truly an "invention factory"—a place in which innovation would take on the routine and reliable character of any other industrial production.

The prevailing trend in modern commerce is streamlining, paring down to essentials. This is one bandwagon Edison would have avoided. He believed that creativity worked best when it was loaded down—purposely overloaded, actually—with an abundance of all that could possibly go into invention, from knowledge to experimental data to machinery to a multitude of *stuff*: elements, compounds, metals, and solvents, synthetic and natural.

5

ENTREPRENEURSHIP

Lesson 33: Take a Reverse Inventory

A traditional inventory is a list of supplies, goods, and merchandise a business has on hand. When Edison set up his first laboratory-workshop in Newark, New Jersey, he sat down with the man who would become his longest-serving assistant and collaborator, Charles Batchelor, and drew up an inventory not of the stuff they had on hand but of things they could make—products that were both feasible and marketable, that not only could be invented but would support the enterprise on which the pair had just embarked. Edison entered the mainstream of his creative career by drawing up an inventory of his creative imagination.

> A good way for a would-be innovator to get started in the business of innovation and invention is to take an inventory of what is possible, feasible, and profitable—an inventory of what as yet does not exist, but that could exist, and, by existing, create profit.

Lesson 34: Identify Markets

Edison formally researched potential new markets, often collecting data on the annual sales of various products that he thought he could improve either in terms of design or in terms of manufacturing method (mainly to reduce production costs). He also kept his eyes open for untapped markets. Toward this end, he earnestly pondered letters he received from friends, business associates, and even strangers suggesting that he get to work on this or that invention. While on his honeymoon in the American South, he even conceived an idea for a cotton picker, and he actually began work on the machine after a plantation owner, James Richardson, wrote specifically asking him to develop one.

> Get into the habit of seeing the world in terms of unserved and underserved markets, a collection of vacuums waiting to be filled.

Lesson 35: Define Yourself

During the inventor's long working life and afterward, a host of critics and commentators debated whether Thomas Edison was or was not a scientist. For Edison himself, there was never any doubt. To a newspaper reporter he famously explained that he was "not a scientific man [but] an inventor," and he went on to explain the difference. "A scientific man busies himself with theory" and is "absolutely impractical," whereas an "inventor is essentially prac-tical." Indeed, Edison declared, the scientist and inventor "are of such different casts of mind that you rarely find the two together." Edison believed that the two outlooks could not "very well co-exist in . . . one man." He continued: "As soon as I find that something I am investigating does not lead to practical results, I drop it. I do not pursue it as a theory." In contrast, a scientist "would be content to go on, and study it up purely as a theory."

> Know what you are about and work accordingly. The entrepreneur of innovation and invention directs all efforts to these two fields, rejecting as incidental everything else.

Lesson 36: Innovate Without Inventing

Edison amazed the world with his inventions, but even the most radically civilization-altering of them were typically innovations based on existing technologies or on analogies with existing technologies. Late in his creative life, beginning in 1927, Edison embarked on a project of innovation aimed at exploiting not an existing technology—but nature itself.

With the automobile industry rapidly expanding, the demand for rubber grew greater every year. Various experimenters were on the trail of methods of manufacturing synthetic rubber. Like these others, Edison saw tremendous potential in the rubber market, but instead of leaping into a quest for an artificial alternative to natural rubber, he turned to nature in a quest for alternative sources of *natural* rubber, using plants available in the United States rather than in far-off climes that were physically challenging and often politically unstable. This late-life project was, in effect, an exercise in innovation without invention—an exhaustive, world-wide research endeavor that eventually encompassed research on 17,000 plant specimens representing 2,222 species. Despite its wide scope—typical of Edison's grind-it-out research method—it was hardly a random effort, but was strategically focused on species known to bear latex. Before he died, Edison narrowed his research to goldenrod, a latex-bearing plant native to the United States that could be harvested like wheat, its rubber content then obtained through the use of chemical solvents. Moreover, goldenrod matured in as little as three months, a much briefer period than many other candidate plants. As it turned out, by the time Edison reached this point in his research, the work others were doing on synthetic rubber was beginning to pay off, and synthetics would prove the more economical alternative to natural rubber.

Although Edison never commercialized a method of extracting rubber from goldenrod, this project from late in the inventor's life offers a powerful lesson: that innovation need not be devoted to creating something from nothing. Instead, it may be a project of transformation and the discovery of alternatives among that which already exists.

Lesson 37: Inspire Confidence

From the beginning of his career, Thomas Edison possessed a gift for inspiring confidence. He did this, first and foremost, by conveying to others the creative energy that animated his own vision. As he compiled a record of one successful invention and innovation after another, he laid an ever-mightier foundation on which the confidence of others was readily built. Moreover, in each project he undertook, Edison maintained a personal presence in every aspect of the creative process, from inception through prototyping and all the way through manufacturing and marketing. He took ownership of the entire project and the entire enterprise.

Yet Edison did not rely exclusively on his record of achievement and his personal charisma to inspire confidence. He came of age in the first great epoch of the American showman—the era of P. T. Barnum and others of his stamp—and he knew the value and power of a strong public image. Edison enthusiastically and skillfully cultivated the popular press by making himself a highly reliable source of exciting news. When reporters portrayed him as the "Wizard of Menlo Park" or the "Modern Prometheus," he raised no false protest of humility—and, in fact, obliged the news writers with more and more stories, including suspenseful blow-by-blow accounts of the progress on this or that impending breakthrough. Similarly, when he left Menlo Park to build a new laboratory–workshop complex in West Orange, New Jersey, he personally sketched the main building. What he drew was a three-story structure incorporating a tower, a very stately mansard roof, and a grand courtyard. His object, he explained to his architect, was to give his "invention factory the dignity of a public building." He wanted it to be an institution. He wanted the public not only to be impressed but to buy into it—to perceive themselves as having a stake in the enterprise that the building housed, just as people felt a certain ownership claim to the U.S. Capitol or the White House.

In the end, brick-and-mortar reality diverged from Edison's initial conception. As it was actually built, the facility at West

Orange resembled a conventional factory more than a grandiose public building. Nevertheless, the impulse to create and maintain an image was a valid one and it endured as a top priority throughout Edison's career. Essential to attracting customers as well as investors, the Edison image was integral to the way he conducted the business of invention and innovation.

> In the real world, creation requires capital, and capital thrives on confidence. An entrepreneur's first invention must be an image that embodies desirable values, projects competence, and compels absolute confidence.

Lesson 38: Take the Credit

The verdict of history is unambiguous: Alexander Graham Bell invented "the telephone." Yet what did this really mean? What was it that he actually invented?

Bell's initial breakthrough was a telephone transmitter in which sound waves vibrated a diaphragm connected to a needle suspended in a high-resistance liquid. The vibration of the needle varied the amount of surface area of the needle in contact with the liquid, thereby varying the resistance and strength of the current passing through the circuit. This variation in electrical current represented the transformation of sound waves into electrical current, which could be reconverted into sound by his telephone receiver.

Bell's liquid transmitter worked, but it did not work all that well. Speech transmitted and received by Bell's telephone was indistinct, and the weak currents produced by the transmitter could not be carried very far. Recognizing the limitations of his equipment, Bell improved his transmitter by linking the vibrating diaphragm to the armature of an electromagnetic relay. As the armature vibrated, it induced a variable current in the coil of the relay. The electromagnetic—or magneto—transmitter was certainly more reliable than the liquid transmitter, but the resulting reproduction of speech was still indistinct and the current, though stronger than with the original system, was still weak.

Although the world was amazed by what Bell had wrought, Edison was unimpressed. He did not begrudge Bell his breakthrough in principle, but it was clear to him that Bell had failed to create a commercially viable product, and his failure to commercialize the telephone gave Edison what he perceived as a very large space within which he could innovate. The carbon button transmitter Edison eventually created addressed the issue of clarity, and the battery power he used to charge the line addressed the issue of the weakness of the current and thereby greatly extended the distance over which the telephone message could be transmitted. Both of these were breakthroughs that made the telephone commercially feasible: a practical consumer product.

History aside, who then should claim the credit for having invented the telephone? The inventor who made the breakthrough in principle? Or the inventor who commercialized the application of the principle?

> Breakthrough discovery is not sufficient for invention and innovation. The practical, profitable application of the breakthrough is what completes the creative cycle.

Lesson 39: Be Legendary

Although his deafness sometimes made Edison appear aloof, he was no temperamental creative hermit. From early in his career, he learned to promote himself by engaging the press, offering juicy stories of forthcoming inventions, inventions in progress, or simply his ongoing research. One reporter called him the "Aladdin's lamp of the newspaper man," adding, "The fellow who approaches him has only to think out what he wants to get before taking the lamp in his hands and he gets it." Reporters relied on Edison to deliver stories they knew would consistently amaze their readers. Virtually everything Edison created—or claimed to be creating—promised to improve the lives of consumers of all kinds. Moreover, while Edison famously asserted that so-called genius was just 1 percent inspiration and the rest hard work and persistence, he nevertheless cultivated in the popular press an image of nearly miraculous genius.

He wanted reporters to present him as the latter-day Prometheus, bringing to the people gifts of unprecedented power. Toward this end, he deliberately blurred distinctions between minor innovations and major inventions, presenting whatever he had in hand as a highly significant breakthrough, even one that might transform civilization itself. Moreover, he freely claimed credit for various inventions in which he had played little or no role, such as the stock printer—a device to which he contributed improvements but certainly did not conceive nor even alter its basic technology. Where the products of his own laboratory–workshop were concerned, Edison never publicly gave credit to any of his small army of employees, experimenters, scientists, and craftsmen (though he sometimes did share patent rights with them). Although he presented himself as the leader of a substantial industrial enterprise, in the matter of invention he encouraged the press to portray him as a lone genius. For their part, reporters were more than willing to do so. The myth of the solitary genius was agreeably romantic and made for compelling narrative. People *wanted* to believe in it, and the press obliged.

Edison a self-promoter? Edison a boaster? Surely it was superfluous for a man who legitimately claimed a steady stream of patents every year, including several for truly life-transforming inventions, to puff himself up in the manner of a showman, but Edison understood that projecting a combined aura of creative genius, absolute self-confidence, and ultimate infallibility was a powerful draw for customers and investors alike. Even with more than enough achievements to back up his grand claims, those claims could always be made grander. After all, who wouldn't jump at the chance to invest in a legend?

Lesson 40: Invent Systems

Edison's great iconic invention was, of course, the incandescent electric lamp. The inventor never regarded it, however, as a stand-alone invention. The electric light was conceived and developed as just one part of a system of electric power generation and application. By inventing practical indoor electric lighting, Thomas Edison was inventing the reason for an entire new utility industry, and work on the lamp proceeded simultaneously with work on generators, electric transmission and distribution systems, and metering systems. The light bulb satisfied a great human need for indoor lighting, but, in satisfying this need, it created a new one: the need for an electric power industry.

The most ambitious and potentially profitable inventions and innovations create—or necessitate the creation of—entire technological and marketing systems. The innovator who, from the beginning, controls as much of the system as possible stands the best chance of realizing the greatest profits. A good salesman makes a sale. A great salesman makes customers. So it is with innovators. The journeyman inventor creates a new device. The great inventor creates a device that both necessitates—and spawns—entire systems.

Lesson 41: Think Bigger

Edison was a keen observer who always studied the details—and yet he made it a practice to think on the largest possible scale, often conceiving the big picture before paying any attention at all to the details. The invention of the incandescent electric light would be a labor of details, especially in the long, painstaking, and exhaustive search for a perfect filament, but the idea of creating a practical electric light did not begin with the filament or even with the entire bulb and filament assembly. These developed inseparably from Edison's initial vision of a lighting—or power—system. From the very beginning, Edison saw the incandescent light as just one part of this system, which, he believed, would ultimately envelop the world. For him, electric lighting was the reason to create a vast, civilization-transforming power system, even as that system would enable the creation of many more electrical devices.

> Never hesitate to think globally, even if you must begin to build locally. Push your thoughts, your plans, your designs beyond individual pieces and into the realm of whole systems.

Lesson 42: Let Research Lead

Thomas Edison identified himself first and foremost as an inventor. In second place was another self-definition—not as a scientist but as a businessman. And just what was the business of this businessman? His business was the business of innovation.

In and of itself, innovation could be the product of inspiration, of whim, or of happy accident. As a business, however, innovation had to be far more regular, reliable, and predictable; it had to be rationalized, and yet it also needed sufficient room for inspiration, for the working of whim and of happy accident. And there had to be room as well for research and experimentation, which might or might not yield immediately profitable results. This being the case, always at the head of Edison's business was the research laboratory–workshop. In many modern industrial firms, the laboratory exists primarily to respond to the needs of production and marketing. In Edison's firms, however, it was the production and marketing departments that followed the work of the laboratory. Edison wanted research to lead everything else.

> If innovation is your business, put innovation in the driver's seat. Although ultimately focused on creating sources of profit, research should be immediately and directly independent of both marketing and manufacturing. Harness the products of imagination, not imagination itself.

Lesson 43: Don't Stop Experimenting

For the pure scientist, experimentation is a passion born of curiosity. For Edison the inventor, it was at least as much a matter of business as it was of passionate vocation. "The only way to keep ahead of the procession," Edison told his chief engineer, William Mason, early in the twentieth century, "is to experiment. If you don't, the other fellow will. When there's no experimenting there's no progress. Stop experimenting and you go backward."

And what if an experiment should fail? In that case, Edison advised experimenting some more "until you get to the very bottom of the trouble."

> The competitive business of innovation requires continual trial, an ongoing program of experimentation—both to come up with new things and to improve current products. Resting your efforts in the manufacture or marketing stage will sooner or later prove fatal to the enterprise. Probably sooner.

Lesson 44: Invite Distraction

Most of us are supremely irritated by distraction. We try to avoid it, and we complain loudly when distraction proves unavoidable. For many of us, a "break in concentration" comes as something of a catastrophe.

But not for Thomas Edison.

The inventor not only invited but sought and welcomed distraction, even when he was most intensely involved in a particular project. For example, during his early intensive experiments with multiple telegraph systems—telegraph systems that would allow multiple messages to be sent and received simultaneously along a single line—Edison freely followed whatever other leads his work on these emerging technologies and devices suggested to him. If he came up with a solution to a problem in one area, he was always open to what possibilities that solution opened up in other areas. If research on one project suggested a new line of research in an entirely different field, he did not even think about suppressing the impulse to strike out in the new direction.

Astronomers have long employed a physiological trick for locating the faintest of the visible stars. Instead of trying to find them in the center of their field of vision, they attempt to catch them out of the corner of an eye. In this part of the human retina, vision is not at its sharpest and clearest, but it is at its most sensitive to low light levels. Similarly, Edison never shunned what he caught at the corner of his eye, even when he was intensely focused on something else. He relished distraction as yet one more creative force.

Lesson 45: Time It

Edison's ultimately failed attempt to make a successful business of electromagnetically separating iron from low-grade ore led to an interest in the possibilities of innovating manufacturing processes to cheaply produce Portland cement of the very highest quality. In part, Edison hoped to recoup a portion of his investment in equipment purchased or built for his iron-refining business by adapting the machinery to cement manufacture. But part of Edison's interest in the cement business was strictly a matter of timing. By 1898, when he began looking into the business potential of making artificial cement—and making it faster, cheaper, and better than anyone else—this commodity was just emerging as the material of choice among a growing number of builders. Edison saw that sales of artificial cement were steadily gaining on those of natural cement, and he determined that the moment for innovation had arrived: it was now—before the market began to mature and while there was still room for newcomers who offered genuine innovation.

> Few inventions are of eternal value. Success in invention and innovation is most often a function of timing, the identification of a cusp moment, when demand for a technology is on the rise or on the verge of a rise and when the technology is established yet not so well established as to preclude significant—patentable and competitive—innovation.

Lesson 46: Imagine the Future

In 1891, the journalist George Parsons Lathrop proposed to Edison that they collaborate on a science fiction novel about the future. Accepting the proposition on the basis that the business of invention is in large part the disciplined art of imagining the future, Edison drew up some hundred pages of notes (though only about a third of these survive) that incorporated many themes from his existing inventions and from ongoing projects. In some of his notes, Edison combined inventions and ideas, imagining, for example, a bare-wire trans-Atlantic cable that used the "etheric force" (a form of electrical energy Edison believed he had discovered) to transmit photographic images from one continent to another. Edison also imagined the perfection of his experiments—in reality, abortive—aimed at producing electricity directly from coal. At this stage in his career, Edison was also becoming increasingly interested in synthetics, and his notes contain ideas for making artificial wood, leather, mother of pearl, diamonds, and silk. Finally, the inventor also inventoried and commented on experimental breakthroughs he knew that other researchers and scientists were working on, including electric cars, high-speed railway transportation, experiments in flight, and even multivalent vaccinations that would prevent a host of diseases. Most spectacularly, Edison speculated on inventions that could alter life on a planetary scale, including vast processes for creating favorable climate change and for accelerating evolution in a certain species of ape.

Ultimately, the literary collaboration did not result in a novel, but Edison's surviving notes provide a unique window into the inventor's imagination, and they suggest that the business of invention and the free-form activity of make-believe have strong roots in common.

Invention is hard work, but it is also play. Ultimately, all inventors and innovators must somehow accommodate the rules and limits of the real world as that world exists and is limited at the moment; however, the most successful inventors and innovators never begin with rules and limits. Instead, they give free rein to the imagination and do not censor their ideas. Cutting and trimming to fit reality should come only after the cloth, in all its wild magnificence, has been woven.

Lesson 47: Get Between

On his visit to the Paris Exposition of 1889, Edison was enthusiastically greeted, feted, and generally hailed. Yet, amid the adulation, he also discovered that the scientists of Europe were always "surprised that I was not more of a scientist." Edison claimed that they "could not understand that I am between the scientific man and the public."

With this phrase—*between the scientific man and the public*—Edison offered a provocative definition of the inventor–innovator.

As he conceived it, the inventor or the innovator operates as a kind of liaison between the world of pure theoretical science and that of the consuming public. As the Greek mythic hero Prometheus, bringer of fire, was a demigod, an intermediary between the godly realm of Zeus and the earthly sphere of humankind, so the inventor was a kind of demiscientist, an intermediary figure between the realm of pure science and that of commerce. Edison the inventor–innovator could afford to slight neither domain, yet, as an inventor, he could not permanently rest in either.

> Inventor–innovators partake of science, of engineering, of manufacturing, of commerce, and of marketing, and yet can specialize exclusively in none of these. Each is always an intermediary, occupying a position of permanent impermanence.

6

CREATING YOUR CUSTOMERS

Lesson 48: Get the News

Edison was a legendary workaholic, but he never let work interfere with reading two morning newspapers and three evening papers as well as devouring "all the principal magazines . . . and most of the scientific publications."

In fact, reading the news was, for Edison, an important part of his work, a key phase of innovation. It is a mistake to think that innovation is all about predicting the future. Successful— profitable—innovation is about engaging the *present*, but doing so at its leading edge. "The news" is a combination of what has just happened and what is happening now. It is neither what has happened in the past nor what will happen in the future. Edison read the news in order to latch on to the leading edge of the present. Innovation does not follow trends—nor does it create them. Instead, it engages them, amplifies them, shapes them, expands them, sustains them, and profits by them. A "young man," Edison wrote, "should always read a daily newspaper" in addition to the journals relevant to his field. "We live and grow by new knowledge."

An innovator need not be a visionary. Indeed, the history of technology is full of the names of bitter and impoverished inventors who "came before their time." As Edison saw it, innovation was all about timing, moving into action neither too late nor too soon. For him, innovation was as current as today's news, neither older nor newer than that.

Lesson 49: Give Praise to the Dissatisfied Customer

The self-taught Edison had a passion for education. He believed that well-educated citizens were essential not only as the creators of an advanced technological civilization but as the consumers of that civilization. He understood that high technology requires not only makers but buyers as well. "If modern industry and invention expected to have a market for its products," Edison wrote late in his life, "it had to turn school-master on an elaborate scale. It had to educate the world before it could sell the world." Edison argued that the purpose of education in a highly technological society was not to create happiness but, quite the contrary, to create among the population a restless dissatisfaction. A society that was satisfied with the status quo could not make progress—that is, it was incapable of acquiring the products of advanced technology. Only when a sufficient number of people had been educated into discontent, so that they demanded new products, would there be an assured place for innovators and inventors. As Edison saw it, the educator had to follow hard on the heels of the inventor, whom he defined as "the specialist in high pressure stimulation of the public imagination," and then the salesman would follow behind both the inventor and the educator to retail what the former had produced and the latter had taught people to want.

Innovation begins with dissatisfaction. It is an itch that demands to be scratched. A few inventors and innovators have the good fortune to stumble across a need that demands satisfying. The vast majority have to create the need—generate dissatisfaction in a particular market—and then set about satisfying it.

Lesson 50: Educate the Customer

The earliest versions of the Edison phonograph were mechanically simple, but they required a certain degree of skill to operate. Edison understood that successfully marketing the phonograph would call for educating customers, in effect endowing them with the skill required to operate the phonograph and derive satisfaction from it. Fortunately, he was able to turn to an existing model to formulate an approach to his program of customer enlightenment. Such consumer devices as typewriters and sewing machines were sold by canvassers who obtained orders, which were then delivered by a functionary typically called an "inspector," whose job it was to install or set up the machine and then provide the user with personalized hands-on instruction. Edison suggested a similar sales and marketing structure for the phonograph, but he did not want the necessity of instruction to scare off potential buyers. Instead of calling his installers "instructors" or even "experts," therefore, he proposed using the more neutral phrase "phonograph operators." The "term 'experts' conveys the idea of intricacy," Edison warned, whereas the use of "Phonograph Operators" would immediately cause "seventy five per cent of the visionary difficulties of the instrument [to] disappear."

> Innovators must surmount various learning curves, including resistance from the established business community, from fabricators, from investors, and—ultimately—from the marketplace, the potential consumers themselves. A quick, comprehensive, painless, and nonthreatening program of education may be an indispensable component of some innovations.

Lesson 51: Learn the Market

Edison the boy was an entrepreneur before he was an inventor, and his subsequent drive to invent was never cut loose from his original entrepreneurial impulse. For Edison, invention always responded to a perceived market and, in turn—provided that it was successful—expanded that market or created new, related markets.

Shortly after he went to work for the Grand Trunk Western Railway as a news butcher, young Tom Edison opened up a pair of stands at the Port Huron railroad station, one selling newspapers and periodicals, the other selling fruits and vegetables. He hired two boys to run the stands, but he finally decided to close both and concentrate exclusively on his train-board business, especially the sale of newspapers. It was a decision entirely motivated by his perception of the evolving marketplace. Developments during the Civil War, especially the catastrophically costly Battle of Shiloh on April 6, 1862, sharply spiked the demand for papers. Edison got ahead of the curve when, arriving in Detroit, he took note of the large crowds pressing around the station bulletin boards that announced the casualties of Shiloh. "I knew that if the same excitement was attained at the various small towns along the road and especially at Port Huron," he later wrote, "that the sale of papers would be great."

It was a keen entrepreneurial perception, and it motivated Edison the inventor—or, more accurately, the innovator—to expand the perceived market even further. As he later explained, "I . . . conceived the idea of telegraphing the news ahead [from Detroit to the smaller towns along the rail line, and I] went to the operator in the [Detroit] depot and in exchange for three months' worth of *Harper's Weekly* [which the young news butcher regularly stocked] he agreed to telegraph to all the stations the matter on the [Detroit] bulletin board," further requesting that all stations copy his transmission. In this way, Edison created a demand for the details behind the headlines announced on bulletin boards all along the Grand Trunk line. His market thus seeded, Edison decided that instead of carrying his usual hundred *Detroit Free Press* newspapers, he would need to stock a thousand. Although he had ready money for no more than three hundred copies, he persuaded the *Detroit Free Press* editor that his scheme was a sure thing, and the man extended credit to the boy.

As it turned out, young Edison actually underestimated his market. At the train's first stop, Utica, a station at which he usually sold two papers, he now unloaded thirty-five. And the trend continued station after station. Unable to adjust to the market with additional quantity, Edison raised the price of the paper from a nickel to a dime, then increased it by five cents at each subsequent station, until, by the time he reached his home, Port Huron, he had but few papers left to sell—at a quarter each. It was an exorbitant price for a newspaper.

Science may be pure, but invention and innovation never are. As Edison seems always to have understood, they are wedded to the market. Yet it is insufficient to say that they respond to the market. Instead, the most successful inventions and innovations coalesce with embryonic markets, then lead, shape, expand, and develop them. Edison saw that there was a market for news, but he also saw that news created its own market. His innovation was to apply technology to leap slightly ahead of the developing demand so that that existing demand was multiplied just in time for him to supply it. Ideally, invention and innovation are no more than a single beat ahead of the market's rhythm.

Lesson 52: Niche Thinking: Find a Small Space to Make It Big

Edison's fame rests on his handful of inventions that transformed civilization: the incandescent electric light, together with systems of power generation and distribution; the phonograph; the improved telephone transmitter; the technology of motion pictures. This is understandable. The larger the arena, the greater the renown. But the vast majority of Edison's thousand-plus patents were for inventions and innovations that hardly aspired to tread the world stage. Most of what Edison patented were highly specialized creations for the niches of technology, including the very niches Edison himself had created. Not only did Thomas Edison produce such niche inventions and innovations throughout his career, it was these specialized creations that were responsible for launching his career in the first place.

As a young telegrapher, Edison began sketching out designs for telegraphic repeaters and for the relays that were the key component of repeaters. Repeaters made long-distance telegraph transmission possible. They worked by receiving a relatively weak signal from a remote transmitter, transferring the transmission to a new circuit, then forwarding it to the next station, whose repeater passed the signal on. This process was repeated, station to station, until the transmission reached its destination. Without repeaters, the current carrying telegraphic transmission would have been too weak to carry very far.

The heart of the repeater was the relay, an electromechanical device that required continual manual adjustment in response to varying conditions along the transmission lines. Edison—along with other creatively inclined telegraphers—was eager to devise a self-adjusting relay, one that would automatically respond to varying line voltage conditions. This work also led him to think about redesigning the entire repeater mechanism for greater efficiency.

The area of telegraphic relays and repeaters was a highly specialized, highly technical niche technology serving a business-to-business rather than consumer market. Innovation in this area required thoroughgoing expertise in a specialized field even to recognize the need, let alone devise the means of solving the problems of the self-adjusting relay. Edison possessed the expertise and created several designs that helped establish him as an inventor. Mastering a specialized field—identifying its needs, problems, and potential—may not only serve to launch a career in invention, it may be sufficient to sustain one. Many successful technological entrepreneurs never set foot in the largest markets. They never had to.

Lesson 53: Offer an Edge

Edison's early inventions exploited niche markets. They consisted of specialized telegraphic applications, a vote recorder for legislative bodies, and, in 1869, the inventor's first significant commercial success: a machine for reporting gold and stock quotations—what was later popularly called the stock ticker.

For gold speculators and stockbrokers, the only commodity more valuable than information was timely information. Indeed, the value of information in any volatile market is directly proportional to its freshness. Edison, who had already learned the lessons of fresh news when he worked as a news butcher on the Grand Trunk and then as a telegrapher along that same rail line, fully understood the relation between information and the premium value of freshness. He readily saw an opportunity in the financial industry's demand for information delivered with maximum speed. Of course, a good many other inventors and telegraphers were aware of this opportunity as well. The gold and stock quotation devices Edison—and others—created were essentially private telegraph systems, by which individual offices were linked. To compete successfully, Edison understood, he would have to offer these increasingly common means of information delivery in a form that was technologically sophisticated but also entirely reliable and very easy to use.

In Boston, Edison achieved a competitive advantage over others offering quotation services by entering the market very early and by offering an apparatus that was elegant in its simplicity and highly dependable. He sharpened and maintained his competitive edge by offering his customers a technological edge as well. His machine, which he called a magnetograph, used a crank magneto to generate the electrical current required to operate it. It therefore required no batteries—an omission that was a major convenience. In Edison's day, batteries were heavy, messy, smelly, and—being filled with sulfuric acid—dangerous. They required frequent charging, and their acid solutions had to be replenished fairly often as well. Eliminating the battery gave Edison a decisive advance on all competitors.

Too often, inventors fall in love with technology and jilt humanity in the process. As Edison saw it, a successful invention was in essence biomechanical: it was not merely a mechanical or electrical device but was, rather, an interface of industrial design with flesh, blood, and brain. It was the middle part of an equation that had mechanism on one side and human beings on the other. Characteristically, his inventions built on existing technology, but they represented an advance on that technology by offering an innovative human interface. A machine, he believed, should give its user a competitive edge—and that meant that the inventor must always give the user the edge over the machine. In the factories of Edison's day, managers spoke of employees "tending the machines." Edison sought a new paradigm, in which machines clearly served their users—and never the other way around.

Lesson 54: Move into a More Hospitable Environment

Like many telegraphers of the 1860s, Thomas Edison was a peripatetic young man, but whereas most operators traveled from job to job, Edison moved from place to place with an eye toward settling somewhere that not only offered work for a telegrapher but that was also hospitable to invention and innovation. Early in 1868, he moved from the Midwest to Boston, which offered everything Edison needed to advance a career in technical innovation. It had a sophisticated technological and scientific community, in terms of both practical industry and academics. It offered great libraries with extensive collections of books and journals devoted to science and industry. Finally, it was also the center of a technologically minded financial community, including money men interested in backing innovations in Edison's favorite field, telegraphy. These were highly specialized venture capitalists, willing to finance experimentation as well as market introduction.

Was Thomas Edison unusually perspicacious in locating so fertile a community? Not at all. As a young telegrapher in the 1860s, Edison was one of a small army of telegraph tinkerers, innovators, and inventors, a number of whom had settled in Boston so that they could obtain venture capital there. Edison followed their lead. It was not a stroke of genius but rather an exercise of acute perception and good, solid common sense.

> Supposedly, when the notorious Depression-era safecracker Willie Sutton was asked why he robbed banks, he replied, "That's where the money is." Like Edison, Sutton identified a community that was hospitable to his profession. Neither for Sutton nor for Edison was this an original idea, but it was a very good one nonetheless.

Lesson 55: Sell Innovation

With each new patent he won, Thomas Edison built the confidence that he could create more advanced technology than any of his competitors, but Edison also understood that "advanced technology" was always a moving target, the product of ongoing innovation; therefore, it was innovation itself that Edison regarded as his edge on the competition. Even more remarkable was the inventor's consciousness that he was working in an age that was coming to value innovation in and of itself. That is, people were beginning to think of innovation as not just a means to an end—a means of making or owning a better, cheaper, more efficient, more beneficial product—but as an end in itself: a product in itself. By the final quarter of the nineteenth century, the great buying public—not only in America, but across the developed world—was coming to value the new precisely because it was new. With a keen instinct for the emerging paradigm, Edison boldly and persistently marketed himself as the Wizard of Menlo Park, the greatest innovator of his age.

As the industrial revolution matured in the late nineteenth century, people came to value innovation for its own sake. The appeal of the new has yet to wear off. The drive to innovate not only creates better products, it satisfies a marketplace hunger for innovation itself. Make innovation. Then sell it.

Lesson 56: The Limits of Innovation

Thomas Edison had a boundless confidence in the salability of innovation. Make it new, he believed, and people would buy it. To a remarkable degree, his faith was well founded. By the end of the nineteenth century and the beginning of the twentieth, the market for innovation was strong. People hungered for new technologies precisely because they were new.

Novelty promised a better life. Nevertheless, even innovation had its limits. The phonograph was a major source of revenue for Edison, sustaining much of his other research and experimentation. Always eager to stay ahead of the competition, Edison threw major resources behind continually improving phonograph technology in the belief that technology alone would defeat the competition. He even declared that the "quality of the records" he produced was far more important than the "reputation of the singers" his company recorded. Although, he admitted, "many people . . . will buy a distorted, ill-recorded and scratchy record if the singer has a great reputation . . . there are infinitely more who will buy for the beauty of the record."

As it turned out, Edison had misread the market. Always more comfortable with selling inventions business to business rather than directly to consumers, Edison blindly assumed that, among consumers, superior technology trumped all other considerations. In the case of business-to-business goods, this assumption was generally a safe bet, but it proved untrue when Edison turned to marketing entertainment directly to the public. Soon enough, Victor and other competitors in the phonograph business were offering recording catalogues with far more attractive material—better singers, more famous instrumentalists, more beautiful, sophisticated, and popular selections—than Edison. Indeed, in a rare departure from his customary prudence, the semi-deaf Edison insisted on taking a personal hand in choosing the music and performers his company would record. He had a strong aversion to musical ornament, including vibrato among string players and vocalists alike. Edison believed that vibrato was intended to cover up a performer's imperfect pitch, whereas genuine connoisseurs of music regarded vibrato as an essential element of beautiful performance. Having misread his customers and having imposed his own questionable musical tastes upon them, Edison found his phonograph business suffering—despite the technical excellence of the machines he produced.

> Technology certainly sells, but it does not automatically trump all other considerations. There is no substitute for thoroughly understanding what your customers want and are willing to pay for. And if what your customers want differs from what you are inclined to give, it is always more profitable to back down, yield to them, and deliver their heart's desire.

Lesson 57: Become a Brand

The "Wizard of Menlo Park" was a wizard of branding. Thanks to his prolific creativity, his development of genuinely civilization-transforming inventions, and his prodigious gift for self-promotion, Thomas Edison succeeded in identifying himself personally with all of the merchandise he marketed. He became a brand, and his characteristic signature, executed with a flourish and duly trademarked, became one of the most recognizable logos in American manufacturing history. The promotion of one invention and innovation after another became all the easier for the personal identification of each with Edison. Prefix his name to any number of products, and they were certain to sell. When his son Thomas Edison Jr. allowed his name to be used to promote a bogus patent electromechanical medical device—a piece of expensive quackery—Thomas Sr. moved quickly. He paid the young man a stipend in exchange for his promise never again to use his name in connection with any product. Edison could not afford to have his trademark—his very identity—compromised.

> Effective branding is an important step in the commercialization of new products. What do consumers want? Simple: They want the impossible. They want something entirely new that they can be confident has worked well in the past. A trusted and familiar brand name on a brand-new product goes a long way toward satisfying this acute contradiction in terms. To sustain innovation in the marketplace, become a trusted brand as quickly as you can.

Lesson 58: No Such Thing as Overproduction

Edison categorically rejected as "nonsense" the idea that "anything which men and women want" could possibly be overproduced. He insisted that the stomach was the "only part of man which can be fully satisfied." In all other respects, human wants are unlimited; they constitute an appetite that can never be appeased.

> Few today can share Edison's faith in the infinite capacity to consume any one product, yet his hyperbole is useful as a guide to invention, innovation, and production. It teaches us to identify those demands that are both greatest and least readily satisfied. On these the successful creative entrepreneurs stake their claims.

7

MAKING RAIN

Lesson 59: Be Skeptical, Never Cynical

People who learn English as a second language are universally appalled by the carelessness with which native speakers pronounce even the commonest words. True enough. English is a loose-fitting tongue. But far more significant than our embrace of a wide variation in pronunciation is our often reckless approach to meaning. Ask most people the difference between skepticism and cynicism, and they will tell you the two words are virtually synonymous or, at least, more alike than different.

They are, of course, quite wrong. Whereas cynics pass through life with a knee-jerk readiness to reject just about everything they see, hear, or even feel, skeptics take in all—but they do so critically, pondering and imagining the potential of each perception and, especially, each piece of received wisdom, critically judging its meaning, its validity, its usefulness. The true skeptic's object is not to reject but to find. Most important, it is to find fertility: approaches, principles, and ideas likely to produce new and useful approaches, principles, ideas.

Samuel Edison, the inventor's father, owned a set of the works of America's archetypal skeptic, Tom Paine, which young Edison recalled first delving into at the especially impressionable age of thirteen. He did so, he said, with a "flash of enlightenment." Paine eloquently and ruthlessly examined and reexamined all that came before him, and, as a result, helped to produce a nation.

As Edison himself explained in later life, he was primed by his early reading of Paine to value free thought, not only as a great liberty—an unalienable right—but as a tool of creative profit. No wonder that Edison contributed an introduction to the collected works of Paine in 1925.

> Millions of feet have trod the same stones over and over again. Stoop to pick some of them up from time to time. Turn them in your hand. Look closely. And then look at what was left behind. Who knows what you will discover? Everything in the world is common, commonplace, and generally useless until someone asks questions, raises doubts, and provokes possibilities.

Lesson 60: Get the Biggest Picture

Throughout his creative life, Thomas Edison invented and innovated a dazzling array of devices for converting energy into useful work. Toward the end of his life, he became increasingly interested in energy itself. By the early 1920s, atomic energy intrigued him because he understood its potential as a force "gigantic and illimitable," capable of producing electricity, he believed, that could be "projected across" not only "the Atlantic, but flung from any part of the world to any other part." Yet he could not visualize this newly discovered force, and he therefore found that he had "nothing to hang the imagination on." In 1922, he reported—vaguely—that he was "experimenting along the lines of gathering information" on atomic energy, but he believed that the actual practical ability to harness it was yet very far off. In the meantime, he thought that titanic forms of energy he *could* see—forms on which he *could* hang his imagination—were even more promising as sources of power. He wrote in 1922 of some day harnessing the motion of the "earth . . . as it turns on its axis and sweeps through space," a force that "would give us all the light, power, and heat that we want, and a thousand times over." He thought, too, that it would be possible to harness the motion of the tides and that science would one day even "imprison the rays of the sun."

The visionary predictions of Edison's old age make for fascinating reading, but the inventor was destined to take no action on these products of his vision. Although many of his inventions did no less than transform civilization, Edison was not primarily a visionary. He was a sometime inventor and a full-time innovator. He built on that which was already in existence, at least in some form. Nevertheless, by the end of his career, his imagination had advanced beyond application to the basis of application. It had expanded from devices to that which animates the devices. Before he died, Thomas Edison took in the bigger picture, the greatest context in which he had long labored.

To criticize Edison for creating energy-transformation devices rather than for working with energy itself is to condemn a human inventor for failing to be a Titan. And yet there is an unmistakable poignancy in reading the inventor's old-age speculations on energy, the vital source behind all that he had achieved. There is the strange sensation that Edison's incredible life of invention had finally come to its epiphany—its great revelation—but the moment had arrived belatedly. In this sense, even the highly successful professional life of Edison is a cautionary tale. Better to take in the bigger picture early in a career than later.

Lesson 61: Design What You Need

Edison sketched entire inventions into his notebooks, but, often, he also filled notebook pages not with whole devices but with components that might be used in any number of devices. Early in his career, for example, when he was developing automatic telegraph transmitters, receivers, and recorders, he poured onto many pages all sorts of designs for a mechanical escapement, a component vital to synchronizing transmission, reception, and recording. The Edison scholar Paul Israel has called this remarkable compilation of designs—which included original designs as well as designs copied from various published sources—a "dictionary of escapements." Edison the innovator was always looking for ways to avoid the labor of creating the utterly new, the radically novel, and the wholly untested. His inventive and innovative practice was to be, wherever possible, evolutionary rather than revolutionary, and much as a writer prefers to use established vocabulary rather than resorting to the invention of new coinages, so Edison compiled his "dictionary of escapements" to speed his work on the various aspects of automatic telegraphy.

Prepare for innovation by acquiring or designing the elements you know that you will need. It is far more economical to compile a vocabulary of innovation durable enough to be used again and again, from one project to the next, than it is to reinvent over and over an entire language of innovation.

Lesson 62: Create New Uses for Whatever You Have

In the 1880s, Edison conducted experiments on what he called a pyromagnetic generator, a device designed to generate electricity directly from coal, in the form of an anthracite (coke) rod, heated with a metal strip in a closed vessel into which a thin gas vapor was injected. The gas would ionize, thereby generating an electric current. The problem, Edison found—and it was apparently insurmountable—was that the heated gas was dangerously explosive. Indeed, after an explosion blew the windows out of a room in his laboratory, he abandoned further experimentation.

When he quit experimenting with pyromagnetic generator, Edison was left with a substantial stock of roasted anthracite carbon, for which he now apparently had no use.

Of course, Edison would never have called any substance useless. As he saw it, nothing was truly useless. His "failed" pyromagnetic experiments, for example, had taught him a great deal about the properties of carbon in various forms, and he took note that the roasted anthracite was far more durable than the brittle substance he was using in what is among his least heralded but most enduringly profitable innovations, the carbon button telephone transmitter. Delving into his "useless" stock of roasted anthracite, Edison further refined his carbon button transmitter to improve long-distance telephone communications, contributing to it's near-century life span.

Edison redefined an innovator as a conserver—one who allowed virtually nothing that passed through his hands and his imagination to be neglected or lost. Whatever he came into contact with, whatever he produced stood as a candidate for experimentation, innovation, or invention. As Edison saw it, an inventor need not create something new if he could create a new use for something old. It was the quality of newness—not the thing itself—that made for innovation.

Lesson 63: "Guard Against Results"

Thomas Edison liked working with men who had proven natural mechanical instincts, who engaged the physical world much as he did: hands-on. One such man was longtime employee John Ott, master machinist. In the spring of 1882, Edison handed Ott sketches of various alternative designs for voltage regulators—part of his emerging electric lighting system—and told him how to get started making them and what results he anticipated from them. But he did not tell Ott to watch for these results or report these results. Instead, he used a phrase heard often in Menlo Park. "Guard against results," Edison cautioned John Ott—and keep careful notes.

In later patent court testimony, Ott explained that to "guard against results" meant to avoid seeing what you expect and to avoid ignoring what you don't expect. In short, it meant being attuned to unexpected results—not because they were errors or failures, but because they were the very results most likely to lead to new inventions, inventions that had not even been conceptualized.

> Focus your work without narrowing your vision. Set a goal, move toward that goal, but open yourself to the distractions of the unexpected, the unbidden, the unwanted. Take note of these for later exploration. Be prepared to wander.

Lesson 64: Exploit the Unexpected

"Guard against results," Edison warned John Ott, one of his most trusted experimenters, meaning that Ott should not allow himself to become so focused on looking for anticipated results that he overlooked or ignored the unexpected results that might point the way to new inventions.

Edison's injunction to Ott points up the powerful aleatoric component in the inventor's method, his openness to randomness, to chance. Personally, Edison possessed the self-confidence not merely to allow himself to be lured down experimental byroads, but actually to invite distraction. Yet sometimes even his vision failed, and he was unable to peer outside the box.

Edison frequently told reporters and biographers that his favorite invention was the phonograph, because it was easy to use and gave unalloyed pleasure to many. Yet Edison's early work on the phonograph—and on the technology of motion pictures as well—had nothing to do with dispensing pleasure, let alone creating an entertainment industry. In the case of the phonograph, the original idea was linked to devices already produced for recording telegraph messages. Edison believed that a device for the recording of the human voice would be useful as a business machine, not unlike the telegraph or the typewriter. The inventor utterly failed to imagine that the phonograph could create and then serve a market for entertainment—a field in which he had no experience and very little interest.

Similarly, Edison imagined that motion pictures would be used primarily for the purpose of education. True, he believed that the kinetoscope could be marketed as a coin-operated peep-show-style entertainment, but it seemed to him that the far larger market would be instructional.

The reason for this failure to conceive—to envision—what now seems the most obvious market for motion picture technology was twofold. First, Edison was familiar with the emerging vending-machine industry, which included a variety of coin-operated devices, including those that exhibited a series of still pictures at the drop of a penny or nickel. Characteristically, Edison innovated rather than invented. That is, he built on existing technologies, markets, and technological systems rather than creating these from whole cloth. Second, Edison was himself a visual learner and a visual creator. Virtually all of his inventions, innovations, and problem solutions began as sketches. He drew out mechanical problems and mechanical solutions to those problems. He also asked his experimenters to make sketches as part of their own notes.

In his later years, when he was widely regarded as an elder statesman of commerce and industry, Edison frequently advocated reinventing America's educational system along visual lines, replacing books in many fields with pictures and motion pictures. He believed that images, not words, were the royal road to the mind. It was, therefore, only natural that he would conceive of movies as a means of teaching and learning.

Edison's uncharacteristically narrow focus simultaneously spurred and retarded the development of both the phonograph and the motion picture. It is not that he conceived the wrong markets for these inventions—after all, Edison made good money from Ediphone business dictation machines, and motion pictures have in fact proven to be superb tools for education—but he was very slow to realize the broadest market: entertainment. Had he envisioned this market from the beginning, the advancement of the phonograph and of motion picture technology would have proceeded faster and would have proven more profitable more quickly.

Imagine all markets. Open yourself to the very markets you never expected.

8

GRINDING IT OUT

Lesson 65: Learn a Lesson from *The Temperate Life*

Edison came of age in an epoch as obsessed with health and diet as our own. It was the heyday of snake oil and patent medicines, of new branches of medicine, and of such philosophers of food and clean living as Post and Kellogg. As for himself, Edison was part of a family that (he said) for three generations had followed the teachings of one Luigi Cornaro in *The Temperate Life*, a manual for healthy living first published in Italy in 1558 and widely translated and reprinted well into the nineteenth century.

Cornaro prescribed many things, but what most attracted Edison was his injunction to experiment with various foods and dietary routines. "By dint of experimenting," Cornaro wrote, "any man may . . . acquire perfect knowledge of his own constitution and of its most hidden qualities, and find out what food and drink, and what quantities of each, will agree with his stomach." In short, the secret of long life and healthy life was not to follow any secondhand pattern or prescription, but to experiment until the ideal fit, unique to you, was found.

Well-meaning parents and teachers often tell children to "find out for themselves" the truths adults already know. Doing this is typically a foolish and hollow exercise, as most youngsters soon discover. Only the most profound truths are individual, specific, and unique to a particular situation, application, or individual. It is these that one must truly find out for oneself, and the only way to do so is by experimentation leading to discovery. The creative life is one of continual trial.

Lesson 66: Know the Known

During the first period of his astounding inventive fertility, the press dubbed Edison the "Wizard of Menlo Park," and reporters avidly sought stories that would give readers a glimpse into his mysterious genius. Valuing publicity as an indispensable adjunct to winning financial backing and building markets, Edison often obliged the newspapermen who routinely visited him at work by favoring them with elaborate progress reports and predictions. Nevertheless, the reality of creation was far more prosaic. Writing in 1914, Edison blandly reported that "When I want to discover something, I begin by reading up everything that has been done along that line in the past—that's what all these books in the library are for."

By definition, innovation cannot occur in a vacuum. Innovation is an improvement on something that already exists. Much the same is true for invention. Theoretically, even without knowledge of existing technology, it is possible to create something entirely new—just as it is possible to pick a winning Wall Street stock by throwing a dart at a list on a board.

It is possible, but it is hardly likely. As with innovation, even the most radical invention typically starts from a thorough knowledge of existing technology.

Know the known. Reap the results of the labor of others. Build on their successes as well as their failures. Define the points of departure, then depart from *them*, rather than starting over at someone else's beginning.

Lesson 67: Want Some Real Labor?
Try Thinking

Over every principal room of his West Orange laboratory–workshop, Edison hung a quotation from the British painter Sir Joshua Reynolds: "There is no expedient to which a man will not resort to avoid the real labor of thinking." Edison complained, late in life, that hardly a day went by when he did not discover the painful truth of Reynolds's maxim.

Edison was a great believer in automation. Machines should and one day would do all the "mechanical" things, he believed, thereby freeing people for creative thought. The trouble was that most people found it more comfortable to behave like machines themselves, spending their time and energy doing mechanical things—going through the usual routines, running in the familiar ruts—rather than straining their mental muscles in genuine innovative thought.

As Edison saw it, digging a ditch was far less work than thinking about ways to make a machine to dig a ditch. He believed that most people were so eager to avoid the hard work of anything like independent thought that they, in effect, cut off their intellect from their eyes, so that the "average person's brain does not observe a thousandth part of what the eye observes." Perhaps Edison believed that this was why there are so few inventors and innovators in the world—and why the few that can be found are regarded as supernatural geniuses. Thought—thought built on careful observation—is the seed of invention and innovation. But thinking is hard work, and the temptation to avoid it is great.

Invention and innovation are launched on thought born of observation. In the absence of either thought or observation, nothing is created.

Lesson 68: "Genius Is 1 Percent Inspiration and 99 Percent Perspiration"

In this, the most famous—and most hackneyed—of his pronouncements, Edison meant to say that so-called genius is mostly an appearance created by hard work.

But there is more to it.

What happens when the inventor–innovator gives free rein to that 1 percent that is inspiration? It is hard to say. The fact is that Thomas Edison rarely did it. Typically, his inspiration began with an analogy to the familiar or an outright adaptation of existing technology and traditional processes. Typically, he innovated rather than invented, improving what already existed rather than creating entirely anew. But when, at the beginning of the twentieth century, he embarked on a radical new design for a rotary roasting kiln to manufacture Portland cement—a kiln much bigger than any in existence and employing a radical "coal gun" technology to fuel it—he allowed inspiration to rule. The result was a behemoth, hardly as famous an invention as the phonograph or the incandescent electric lamp, but a truly impressive piece of machinery nevertheless. Yet because it was such an imaginative leap beyond the state of the industry's art, Edison had no existing technological springboard from which to start. Only by exhaustive trial and error were he and his assistants able to formulate the optimum methods and practices for operating the kiln. Edison intended to produce 1,000 barrels of artificial cement daily (compared to the 150 to 200 barrels existing kilns produced), and it took three years of experimentation before this goal was actually reached. That was a great deal of perspiration indeed.

The more radically an innovation departs from existing technology, the more difficult and time-consuming will be the process of perfecting it—that is, of discovering its potential and its limits. This is an argument for favoring innovation over invention whenever possible. Yet it is by no means a sovereign argument. Some things simply cry out to be invented from the ground up.

Lesson 69: Work the Problem

Edison's secret for productivity was really quite simple. He never stopped working. When he came up against a wall in the course of developing an invention, he worked the problem. In 1904, for example, he found that some cells of his newly developed storage batteries exhibited—spontaneously, it seemed—an unexplained loss of capacity to hold a charge. Because the batteries were already in production, he called a temporary halt to manufacturing—he did not want bad batteries poisoning the market for his product—and he devoted two laboratory rooms, staffed by eighteen experimenters, to solving the problem. This special unit worked day and night until the source of the problem was discovered and corrected.

Because Edison was already marketing his batteries, he decided that he had no choice but to work the problem intensively until it was solved. He believed it was very bad business indeed to knowingly put a faulty product before the public. When knotty problems were encountered at earlier, preproduction stages of innovation, Edison did not always or automatically throw all resources into solving the difficulties. Sometimes, he turned from the recalcitrant project to work on another, different project—then he returned, with a fresh perspective, to the original. The point is that, whether he worked the problem or worked on a different project, Edison never called a halt to the work itself.

Problems are part of business. Either solve them or move on to something else. The one alternative that is the death of business is idleness. Keep working.

Lesson 70: Redesign

In August 1869, Edison was hired as superintendent of Laws's Gold and Stock Reporting Company of New York City. Samuel Laws had pioneered telegraphic gold and stock quotation in the financial capital, and he was very successful at it; however, looking over his shoulder, he could see the upstart Calahan's Gold and Stock Telegraph Company gaining on him. There was a good reason. Whereas Laws offered only an indicator device, Calahan had a full-scale printer.

In response, Laws designed a printer of his own, but he ran afoul of the patent Calahan had secured. Edison stepped in to redesign the printer primarily to overcome the obstacle of patent conflict. In the process, however, he genuinely improved the device by simplifying its mechanism, reducing the number of moving parts, and also trimming down the machine's size. Additionally, Edison introduced two significant mechanical innovations: a wheel replacing the ink ribbon and a more sophisticated electromagnetic mechanism to maintain synchronization between the printer and transmitter. Edison's innovations were hardly revolutionary, but they were sufficiently original to merit patent protection and to draw customers away from the competitor. His innovation was no more extensive than it had to be.

> Competition is a powerful spur to innovation, but beating the competition does not always call for radical technology. Build on existing technology. It is good to introduce overall improvements (in Edison's case, a more efficient machine), but best of all to incorporate significant, discrete, marketable improvements (the ink wheel and electromagnetic synchronization).

Lesson 71: Don't Stop with Version 1

To create the prototype of his incandescent electric lamp, Thomas Edison conducted thousands of experiments, most of them in search of the best filament material. Even if we consider the prototype version 1 of the invention, we would be justified in concluding that, as the product of so much trial and error, experimentation, and tweaking, this "version 1" was already a prime candidate for mass production.

Not that Edison viewed it this way.

In the spring of 1884 alone, he supervised 2,774 more lamp experiments at Menlo Park prior to authorizing the beginning of mass production. The cost of the experiments was $70,000, each of them aimed at refining every detail of design and manufacturing in order to produce low-cost, long-lived lamps capable of several levels of candlepower, depending on the desired application. Even after manufacturing began, experiments intended to produce additional improvements and economies continued at an approximate cost of $1,000 per month.

Be wary of the "Eureka!" moment. Cast a cold eye on your discovery and a critical eye on your prototype.

Lesson 72: The Two Masters

Those who would earn their bread by invention must be resigned to serving two masters, one technical, the other economic. More than once, Edison found that he had arrived at a technically feasible solution to a problem, only to discover that the solution did not address economic considerations. For example, he found that cadmium was an excellent substitute for lead as a battery electrode. It was much lighter than lead and was far less subject to corrosion and erosion. In economic terms, however, cadmium presented a serious drawback. Whereas lead could be had for 4 cents a pound, the cost of a pound of cadmium was $1.20. The obvious means of closing this gap, Edison believed, was to find a cheap source of cadmium, but when this effort finally failed, the inventor had no choice but to abandon cadmium and look for another substance that satisfied both the technical and economic requirements. He did not complain about being frustrated, nor did he raise the cost of his battery. Instead, he acknowledged economics as one of the two masters he was obliged to serve, took a breath, and resumed his research.

> Your enterprise cannot afford to take out a mortgage on an ivory tower. Each and every innovation must satisfy economic as well as technological requirements. Whatever else it may be, innovation must be affordable—capable of being clearly perceived as a good value.

Lesson 73: Try a Kaleidoscopic Approach

Well-meaning parents and teachers tell us to finish one thing before we begin another. It is advice so common that it is seldom questioned. Edison rejected it outright.

No one attacked a problem as persistently as Thomas Edison, but he always worked simultaneously on multiple projects. An attorney for Western Union, under whose auspices Edison worked early in his career, marveled at what he called his "remarkable kaleidoscopic brain. He turns that head of his and these things come out as in a kaleidoscope, in various combinations, most of which are patentable."

Edison was both stimulated and refreshed by working on more than one project at once. Moreover, this kaleidoscopic approach often allowed him to get a fresh purchase on a project that had reached an apparent dead end. Instead of becoming frustrated or, even worse, discouraged, he could simply "put . . . aside [the recalcitrant project] and get at something else." The result, as often as not, was that the very idea he had wanted for the original project would suddenly come to him, unbidden. When it did, Edison would "drop the other and go back to it and work it out." Moreover, the multiple-track approach often resulted in cross-fertilization, as ideas and experience gained from working on one project productively influenced work on another.

As Edison tackled several projects simultaneously, so he tended to invent simultaneous multiple variations on a solution to a particular problem. "I do not wish to confine myself to any particular device," Edison jotted more than once in his notebook records of work on various problems. Indeed, it was rare that Edison would sketch a device and then immediately proceed to build it. More often, he sketched multiple approaches to a problem, one after another, then turned over some or all of the sketches to his experimental and fabricating teams. He usually wanted to see more than one prototype.

> If innovation is a force, why restrict its flow to a single channel? Exploit parallel, intersecting, and multiple courses for your creativity.

Lesson 74: Exploit the Details

Faced with inventing not just an electric light, but the entire electric lighting system of which the light was to be only one part, Edison could be forgiven if he had failed to take note of and address every last detail of what amounted to a massive, complex invention. He could have been forgiven, but he would never have forgiven himself.

Even as he struggled to find a durable filament for his light and a workable design for a generator, Edison pondered the economics of the entire electric lighting system. He reasoned that interior electric lighting would be used primarily at night, which meant that the load—the demand—on any electric generating and distributing system would be substantial at night but comparatively sparse during the day. How, he asked himself, could the load be balanced? After all, it would be difficult to make the monumentally expensive creation of an entire infrastructure quickly profitable if the entire investment was for all practical purposes idle during twelve of every twenty-four hours. The answer, Edison believed, was to market electric motors as aggressively as electric lighting. He wanted to produce motors to run elevators and manufacturing machinery of all kinds—devices that would be used more in the day, during regular working hours, than at night. If the electric light was the must-have appliance for the hours of darkness, why couldn't the electric motor enjoy similar demand during the day?

In the thick of resolving a host of technical problems involved in creating a whole new industry and, indeed, way of life, it is a wonder that Edison gave such thorough thought to a problem of the economics of operation. That he did suggests Edison was loath to separate the technological from the economic dimensions of his inventions. Everything he created had to earn its keep, and that was a problem he never put off resolving.

> When innovating entire systems, you can afford to postpone consideration of no critical detail. Parallel development is crucial in the profitable creation of devices with multiple components or systems with multiple devices. Serial development risks imposing a period of nonproductive dormancy on whatever pieces of the invention emerge first. Such a linear approach also invites problems of compatibility, increasing the odds that component A, completed on Day 5, will fail to work well with component B, completed on Day 300. Defer the details at your peril.

Lesson 75: Speed

In his early teens, Tom Edison learned the rudiments of telegraphy from the Grand Trunk stationmaster in his hometown of Port Huron, Michigan. With this knowledge under his belt, he went on to teach himself the Morse code. For the purposes of practicing sending and receiving, he built a telegraph key and set as his goal not only gaining mastery of the code but building facility and velocity. Thus speed became one of the goals of Edison's professional life.

After just three months of intensive practice, Edison was a sufficiently adept telegrapher to get a job at Micah Walker's store in Port Huron, which doubled as the Western Union telegraph office. For Edison, the job's most attractive perk was having access to the books and magazines—including an impressive array of scientific magazines—that were among Walker's wares. Edison had to cram his reading into his off hours and before the books and magazines of interest to him were sold to paying customers. He therefore formulated his own method of speed reading, deliberately training himself to see words in clusters or blocks rather than individually, so that he could take in the most meaning in the shortest possible time.

> Be omnivorous. Be greedy. Take in as much as possible. The faster you can take things in, the more you can swallow. The more general knowledge you possess, the more quickly and efficiently you can research problems and innovate solutions. Speed buys time, and time fuels invention. "Anything which tends to slow work down," Edison wrote in 1926, "is waste."

Lesson 76: Plod

Despite his love of speed, Edison was never too proud to plod, and the most famous example of Edison's prodigious plodding was his worldwide search for the best material out of which to fashion filaments for his electric light. Thousands of substances were collected and tested, it is true, but this does not mean that Edison's plodding was aimless and without plan. At one point, he had impregnated horseshoe-shaped pieces of cardboard with lampblack (carbon) and used them as filaments. They worked, but their useful lives were short. Instead of blindly groping after a better material, Edison studied the cardboard under a microscope in an effort to understand just why the material had proved unsatisfactory.

After close examination, he concluded that paper would never be much good for a practical filament because the microscope revealed that its fibrous structure "looks like a lot of sticks thrown together." In some places, the "fibres are packed," but in others there are "few fibres, dense spots and great open holes." This irregularity of structure, Edison reasoned, fatally shortened the working life of any paper-based filament. He declared to his staff his belief "that somewhere in God Almighty's workshop there is a vegetable growth with geometrically parallel fibres suitable to our use. Look for it." Although there were, in fact, thousands of substances that exhibited more or less parallel structure, Edison's instructions, based on close observation and analysis—a drive to understand the properties of whatever he worked with—nevertheless narrowed down the candidate materials from hundreds of thousands or even millions of substances to a few thousand. It was a start.

> Not only can a thinker be a plodder—sometimes, thinkers make the very best plodders.

Lesson 77: Unlimited Incentive

Edison always aimed innovation at practical profit, yet making a living was never the sole driver—and perhaps not even the principal driver—of his work. In a 1914 critique of socialism, he observed that, whereas the capitalist system offered the compelling social and economic incentives of competition for profit, socialism, which lacked the profit motive, would have to provide some other "unlimited incentive for its executive minds and its creators" if it were to succeed in maintaining a high level of technological civilization. This observation seems to have provoked a further burst of introspection: "Unlimited incentive. The motive I have for inventing is, I guess, like the motive of the billiard player, who always wants to do a little better—to add to his record." In short, invention, for Edison, was its own reward. As a man of business, Edison was keenly aware of competitors, but his chief competition was himself. As for the profits derived from invention, the inventor typically used the proceeds derived "from one invention to make experiments looking toward another invention." With remarkable candor, Edison declared that if "socialism gave me the means to continue inventing, I would invent; but if it failed to do so, or began to tie me down, I would quit."

> The prime mover of invention is an "unlimited incentive" that flows from within: a drive to excel. As the example of Edison demonstrates, however, this prime mover—invention driven for the sake of invention, the technological equivalent of "art for art's sake"—is entirely compatible with invention for profit. There is no law, social or natural, that says you cannot love what you do and still make money at it.

Lesson 78: If At First You *Do* Succeed, Try Again Anyway

History describes Thomas Edison as an inventor. He described himself—far more accurately—as an inventor–manufacturer. Unlike many so-called independent inventors, Edison rarely sold or even licensed his major inventions and innovations to established manufacturing firms. Instead, he almost always took on himself the commercialization, manufacture, and marketing of whatever he created. This was not merely an act of egocentricism; it flowed from a belief that controlling all aspects of creation, production, and marketing was the best business deal. "The patents I am now taking," he told investors in the Edison Electric Light

Company Ltd. of London, "are more valuable than those already taken. Those already taken were to secure if possible the science of the thing. Those I am now taking are commercial."

Yet there was more to Edison's need to control all aspects of creation—from inception to design to prototype to commercialization to manufacture to marketing. By working hands-on to make and market his creations, Edison found that he could continually innovate upon his own work, even reinvent his inventions, making them more efficient, more reliable, more economical. For this inventor, no invention was ever finished, even after it had been successfully marketed for years.

Edison accepted failure as a learning opportunity, a chance to gather the data that would ultimately drive success. Certainly, he would not have argued against the maxim, "If at first you don't succeed, try, try again." However, initial failure or initial success were, for him, equally inconclusive. Whatever the result, Edison almost always tried again—either in the laboratory or in the process of manufacturing and even long after a product was marketed. The experiment was never concluded. Invention was a means of doing business.

9

MANAGING

Lesson 79: Never Neglect Logistics

For Edison, there were no purely theoretical, technical, or creative problems. Invention was a continuous process, a spectrum, and no phase of invention could be walled off from another. Always working with an eye toward commercialization, he never neglected the logistical dimension of invention. When he concluded that platinum was one of the more technically promising materials for light bulb filaments, he did not close his eyes to the expense of the metal—he immediately set about searching for plentiful sources of it. Even as he searched, he continued to look for cheaper alternatives to platinum—eventually hitting on lampblack, or carbon, which could be produced cheaply and in great plenty.

> What works in the laboratory must be made to work in the marketplace. The question, "Can this be made?" must be followed—without delay—by two more questions: "Can we make this?" and "Can we sell this?"

Lesson 80: "Mean to Succeed"

By the time he was working on a new design for a generator to power his electrical lighting system, Thomas Edison possessed a keen insight into his own inventive process. He wrote to his European agent, Theodore Puskas: "I have the right principle and am on the right track, but time, hard work, & some good luck are necessary, too."

How did he know these things? From experience.

"It has been just so in all my inventions. The first step is an intuition and comes in a burst. Then difficulties arise. This thing gives out, then that. 'Bugs,' as such little faults and difficulties are called, show themselves. Months of intense watching study & labor are required before commercial success—or failure—is certainly reached."

Edison drew on his experience of the creative process to carry him through the difficult and doubtful span that separates original concept from commercialization. He even admitted the possibility that the end result might be commercial failure—although that eventuality was clearly subordinated to what he took as the greater likelihood of success. He capped his comments to Puskas by assuring him that "before I have done with it I mean to succeed."

> *Mean to succeed.* It is a telling phrase that reflects a frame of mind and a will calculated to carry a project through long trials to ultimate success. Begin with the intention of succeeding, and shape all that you do toward that intended goal. This includes cherishing and sustaining, through all difficulties, the spark of the original conceptual intuition.

Lesson 81: Plan for Spontaneity

Free association and spontaneously occurring notions are valuable sparks and catalysts for creativity. They can't be forced, but they can be induced, encouraged, and planned for.

When Edison was starting out in his Newark, New Jersey, laboratory–workshop, he spontaneously sketched inventions and components on whatever scrap of paper happened to come to hand—and he encouraged his employees to do the same. This proved so valuable a source of ideas that Edison regularized the practice by deliberately placing notebooks throughout the work-space. By the time he moved into his Menlo Park facility, Edison "commenced the practice of placing note books all over my labora-tory, with order to my assistants to draw out and sign every experi-ment." Finally, by 1880, he began assigning specific notebooks to particular projects, rather than randomly distributing them throughout the shop. The evolution from scraps to notebooks to organized notebooks marks a progress from pure spontaneity to regulated—planned—spontaneity.

> Spontaneity is a powerful force. Do what you can to capture it without killing it.

Lesson 82: Create a Shop

Edison's laboratories—in New Jersey as well as in Florida—were more accurately described as laboratory–workshops. They had about them as much of the appearance of a machine shop as of a scientific research laboratory. There was good reason for that. From the beginning, when he set up his first full-time research facility in Newark, New Jersey, under the auspices of the Newark Telegraph Works, he drew up a contract that specified the provi-sion of machine shop facilities as part of his "laboratory." Earlier, in Boston and New York, he had been frustrated by having to wait for outside machine shops to fabricate or modify parts and even entire devices for him. He resolved that henceforward he would always make sure that he had support for his own fully staffed machine shop wherever he worked.

It was a crucially important idea, because it enabled Edison to create, test, and modify inventions rapidly, cheaply, and (when nec-essary) under his direct supervision. Yet it was not an original idea. Other mechanical inventors maintained their own machine shops, sometimes occupying downtime by contracting or subcontracting for small-scale manufacturing when the shop was not engaged in experimental work. In integrating a machine shop into his laboratories, Edison was not trying to be original. He took good ideas wherever he found them, and any idea that improved the speed and flexibility of creative development was a good idea.

> The more of the creative process you can directly control, the better. Take steps to reduce the layers separating concept from prototype. This will save time and facilitate efficient experimentation. Do not hesitate to study and to borrow the "best practices" of others in your field—or outside your field, for that matter.

Lesson 83: Start a School

As Edison pushed ahead with the commercialization of his electric lighting system, marketing electrification to industry, communities, and entire cities, he encountered—not surprisingly—a terrible dearth of experienced electrical engineers, electricians, installers, and other workmen to do the necessary building, installing, maintaining, and operating of the components of the system. The wiring of buildings was often undertaken by plumbers, whose vocation was at least roughly analogous to that of the emerging trade of electrician, but Edison well knew that this stop-gap was hardly sufficient to the needs of the vast industry that was rapidly taking shape under his hands. Edison approached Columbia University in New York City about establishing an electrical engineering program, and he consulted with other colleges and universities throughout the nation in an effort to create interest in setting up relevant curricula.

But the academic institutions moved at a pace far more sedate than the pressures of commercialization could tolerate. Edison therefore established his own school, transforming what had been the equipment testing room of his Goerck Street facility in lower Manhattan into a genuine academy for his electrical workers. The program was complete with a formal curriculum and carefully prepared written examinations. As Edison's electric lighting business grew, one of his staff, Charles Clarke, opened a dedicated school farther uptown, at 65 Fifth Avenue, and even wrote a textbook specifically for the student-employees.

> Edison's schools were in themselves an innovation, and they profoundly influenced the emerging electric power industry. Throughout the nation, new electric power companies followed the Edison model in setting up formal training programs. It was, therefore, the industry itself—not the academic community—that created the first generation of practical electrical engineers, electricians, and electrical workers. An innovator is an innovator, creating new products, new markets, and even new workers. Sometimes innovation must be thrust into all dimensions. Sometimes it must be made to create a new world.

Lesson 84: Make Creativity a Predictable Process

Edison came to hold over a thousand patents, but he could not patent what was perhaps his single most significant invention: his own creative method. That was an innovation that shattered two enduring and pervasive patterns of production. The first was the long-held and rarely challenged belief that industrial production was incompatible with individual craftsmanship. The second was that invention was essentially born of inspiration and furthered by genius and was therefore entirely unpredictable. To overcome these crippling mythologies, Edison established at Menlo Park, New Jersey, what he called an "invention factory." It combined laboratory, workshop, and factory, and it employed scientists and craftsmen who were expected to solve the problems Edison set for them, but to do so in a democratic and informal atmosphere that allowed them the space to exercise their own initiative. In contrast to most industrial-age employers, Edison did not want men who served machines or who worked like machines. A hundred men thinking the same way and doing the same thing was hardly productive, as Edison saw it. Instead, he wanted a hundred men thinking and doing on their own, but focused on the goals and objectives he set for them. His leading idea was to focus creativity even while multiplying it. In this way, Edison believed that he greatly improved the odds of creating one successful invention after another. And that was the very business of an "invention factory."

Like so many of Edison's inventions and innovations, the "invention factory" approach seemed quite radical, and yet it was deeply rooted in existing technologies and traditions. Menlo Park was far more a community of craftsmen than it was a factory town. It harked back to an era before the advent of mass production. Within the culture of craftsmanship that Edison fostered, he encouraged his workers to be "muckers." It was a term he and his men borrowed from the British working class, and it was related to the verb phrases "to muck in" or "to muck about"—in other words, to fool around, to have fun. As used in the Edison "invention factory," the term *mucker* was admittedly a bit disingenuous. After all, the Menlo Park muckers did not fool around idly—but they did fool around within the parameters of whatever task Edison set for them. The inventor once observed that no device of any real value worked by itself; instead, "You got to make the damn thing work." That, in effect, was his single injunction to the muckers. *How* they made it work was, typically, entirely their business.

Not that Edison washed his hands of project management. His roles in the "invention factory" were as mastermind—the chief source of invention, the setter of goals—and as the one who apportioned tasks, assigning one aspect of an invention to one "gang" (his term) of experimenters and machinists and another to another gang. This done, he gave his workers great latitude in accomplishing their assigned tasks and solving all of the problems attendant on those tasks. When he monitored their work, he did so in a strictly collegial manner, sharing rather than imposing ideas and often serving as a liaison between the various working gangs. The idea was to keep production going, both creatively and reliably.

> To rationalize creativity without killing creativity is challenging, but it is by no means a contradiction in terms. Sport—which is organized play, play with rules, play with goals, play with accounting (called scorekeeping)—is still undeniably play. Intelligently managed, creativity becomes invention and innovation—that is, creativity with rules, goals, and accounting.

Lesson 85: Create Standards

Edison relished informality and cultivated the individual initiative engendered by a craft shop culture. He knew, however, that his enterprise ultimately had to exist within the greater culture of an industrial society, a marketplace that had come to expect and demand the reliability, uniformity, and availability of technology created by mass production. Thus Edison divided the innovative research efforts of his company into invention on one hand and manufacturing on the other. For example, he created an internal "Standardizing Bureau" to create standards for all equipment used in the Edison electric lighting system. The bureau did not simply impose its standards, it took into consideration the input of "the experimenter, the manufacturer and the practitioner" to create the most efficient, useful, and economical standards possible, standards intended to fully address the needs and concerns of all stakeholders in the Edison system. In addition to soliciting and collating stakeholder opinion, the Standardizing Bureau commissioned and reviewed general research into the best methods of manufacture and design. The bureau continuously evaluated all parts of the system.

> Creativity resists the imposition of arbitrary rules and regulations, but it is not incompatible with efforts at standardization for uniform excellence, provided that intelligently formulated, clearly articulated standards are presented as just one more set of criteria any invention or innovation must meet. Standards should be integrated into the creative process rather than imposed upon it as a test after the fact of creation.

Lesson 86: Subdivide, Delegate, Empower

In one of many contemporary news stories that peered into the workshop of the Wizard of Menlo Park, the *New York Herald* in January 1879 depicted what it called a reversal of the "ordinary rules of industry" at the Menlo Park complex. "At six o'clock in the evening the machinists and electricians assemble in the laboratory. Edison is already present, attired in a suit of blue flannel, with hair uncombed and straggling over his eyes, a silk handkerchief around his neck, his hands and face somewhat begrimed and the whole air that of a man with a purpose and indifferent to everything save that purpose." Carelessly attired, somewhat grimy, Edison appeared to be just another workman in the shop. As the "hum of machinery drowns all other sounds and each man is at his particular post," Edison himself "flits about, first to one bench, then to another, examining here, instructing there; at one place drawing out new fancied designs, at another earnestly watching the progress of some experiment."

To the *Herald* writer, this all seemed a radical departure from the prevailing practices of American industry. And indeed it was. But what he saw was not a radical innovation in research and prototyping, but something that harked back to an age before mass production, an age of craftsmanship. Edison ran his Menlo Park workshop–laboratory in the spirit of a craft culture, in which each of the key workers was a highly skilled craftsman—machinist, electrician, chemist, whatever—who was given an assignment, but, within the requirements of the assignment, was also permitted great latitude and autonomy and was, in fact, positively encouraged, even required, to experiment. Edison explained that he would assign a problem to what he called a "gang of one good experimenter and two or three assistants." The experimenter managed the gang and proceeded with little interference from Edison, who would do no more than "flit" by from time to time. On at least one occasion, the leader of a gang, stymied by a problem, asked Edison what he should do next. "Don't ask me," the inventor replied. "If I knew I would try it myself."

The craft culture was by no means as laissez-faire as it appeared to the *Herald* writer. To be sure, it was a loose, unregimented style of production, but it was very intensely task oriented. Edison never relinquished the role of master manager. As the writer reported, "Sometimes he hastily leaves the busy throng of workmen and for an hour or more is seen by no one. Where he is the general body of assistants do not know or ask, but his few principal men are aware that in a quiet corner upstairs in the old workshop, with a single light to dispel the darkness around, sits the inventor, with pencil and paper, drawing, figuring, pondering. In these moments he is rarely disturbed. . . . He is in the throes of invention." As longtime assistant John Ott put it, Edison "was as dirty as any of the other workmen, and not much better dressed than a tramp." Yet he was clearly the leader of the enterprise: "But I immediately felt there was a great deal to him," Ott observed of his first encounter with Edison. One moment he was one of the boys, the next an aloof inventor, drawing up the assignments he would distribute to his craftsman gangs.

Edison perfected a creative method that gave him intimate contact with hands-on experimentation, prototyping, and production, yet also allowed him the isolation to invent. He hired craftsmen on whom he could rely to exercise informed initiative within the parameters of whatever he assigned. He was thus able to subdivide and allocate the various aspects of a project, so that work could advance on several parallel tracks.

The culture of craftsmanship Edison fostered not only accelerated creative development, it created satisfaction and loyalty among his workers, who eagerly put in eighty-hour weeks. Edison's personal leadership generated camaraderie. Whenever the pressure threatened to become too intense, Edison himself would call a recess, taking his men fishing—for Menlo Park was then a rural place—and even hiring a musician to play a pipe organ that occupied one end of the shop. Edison was a driven worker himself, yet he rejected the Protestant work ethic as it was traditionally conceived. For him, the work of invention and innovation partook of play. It was hard, yet it was fun. And that is the version of the work ethic he instilled at Menlo Park.

> The creative leader sets tasks, goals, and provides direction—then steps back, monitoring progress in a collegial rather than dictatorial manner. The workshop should be a playroom, albeit with the play focused sharply on a creative end product.

Lesson 87: Harvest Complaints

Edison avidly devoured feedback from his customers, especially the complaints. In these he found his inspiration and guidance for innovation and improvement. When one of his key associates, Francis Upton, neglected customer complaints concerning faulty lamps, Edison scolded him for not having learned "the Lamp business ie the Carbonization of filaments." The "financing is rather easy," Edison wrote in a note to him. "I suggest you do like the rest of us learn the business thoroughly & not be dependent on others = you are degenerating into a mere business man—Money isn't the only thing in this mud ball of ours."

A successful business may be built on the complaints of customers, provided they are harvested productively. This requires a thorough knowledge of your business, bottom to top, as well as a commitment to excellence, quite apart from turning a dollar.

Lesson 88: Favor Fluid Structures

As a young telegrapher, Edison always bid to secure working the night shift—which he generally got, because nobody else wanted to work it. "Night jobs suited me," Edison recalled late in life, "as I could have the whole day to myself."

From the beginning of his working life, Edison refused to be governed by the rising and setting of the sun or by conventionally accepted working hours. His day was fluid, and, like Napoleon, he cultivated the habit of catnapping, grabbing a few minutes of sleep here and there throughout the day and the night, sitting in a chair, lying on a work table—or sometimes lying under the table. He refused to stifle the productive pressure of creative work. Instead, he arranged his day—and his night—to make room for his ideas and their realization.

Yield to the flow of creative thought. Do you want to innovate? Begin by innovating the outworn structures of your workplace and workday.

Lesson 89: Keep Score

There can be no doubt that Thomas Edison took great joy in the creative processes of invention, yet he was always determined to make invention a business, and he knew that the language of any business is spoken in time and in money. Creativity is a force he was loath to fetter, but, as a businessman, he was committed to keeping score.

Edison called for "a better time sheet . . . for the Experimenters. Something which describes [the] nature [of the] experiment, time consumed & Roughness of amount of material used. . . . Also we must apportion the rent of different parts of Laboratory." Edison assigned every project a number so that the project's costs and revenues could be readily tracked.

Among the coterie of his closest assistants were master machinists, glassblowers, chemists, physicists, electrical engineers, and general craftsmen. In addition to these experts, there was also one William Carman, a brilliant young accountant. A successful invention, Edison believed, not only got its job done, it did it simply, elegantly, and economically. A successful "invention factory"—which is what he termed his enterprise at Menlo Park, New Jersey—likewise had to give maximum latitude to innovative creativity, but it had to operate in a way that made good business sense. This meant that the customary method of keeping books in the traditional industrial workshop—a means of accounting for the man-hours and materials used on each job—provided an insufficient record for analyzing the economy of Edison's invention factory. Carman created a new accounting system, which tracked expenditures on various aspects of various projects, with particular emphasis on the allocation of the factory's most valuable commodity: the labor of its specialized craftsmen, scientists, and engineers. Each employee was issued a gridded sheet, with the days of the week on the vertical axis and columns for each project or project phase on the horizontal axis. Each worker noted the number of hours spent on each project or phase of a project. Wages were readily calculated by simply adding the horizontal rows, while project costs could be analyzed by adding the vertical columns. The accounting method provided a vivid cost picture of each project and allowed intelligent decisions to be made about allocation of resources as well as the profitability of any given project.

Innovative creativity is a driver of great businesses, but, in the context of a business enterprise, creativity must be made to speak the language of business. Whatever else the collective creativity of an enterprise produces, it must also produce a record of its processes in terms of labor, time, and material costs clearly broken down by project and project phase. No intelligent decisions regarding the value of research, prototyping, and start-up production efforts can be made without such an accounting.

10

FAKING GENIUS

Lesson 90: Model It

Before embarking on any large-scale invention or innovation, Edison devoted considerable effort to modeling solutions to problems in an effort to "pre-determine the probabilities of success or failure of [a planned] device." Modeling consumed time, effort, and cash, but it potentially saved much more of each than it cost. In the late 1880s, when Edison worked diligently on the electromagnetic extraction of iron from low-grade ore, he was faced with the problem of having to experiment with some aspects of his proposed process that proved impossible to model. The means by which the ore was crushed prior to being passed through the electromagnetic separator proved to be a critical phase of the process—yet Edison discovered that attempts to model large-scale crushing machinery using smaller and cheaper devices "gave no indication as to whether or not the larger [equipment] would be successful." The only alternative, therefore, "was to boldly start on the experiment [at full scale], realizing the fact that if it failed we would lose many thousands of dollars." In the end, Edison did indeed fail to produce a commercially viable method of electromagnetically separating iron from low-grade ores, and the entire attempt, which consumed more than a decade and hundreds of thousands of dollars, was widely dubbed "Edison's folly."

> Hedge development costs by means of a dedicated modeling program. In the absence of models—or when useful modeling proves impossible—risk is significantly increased. The larger the proposed project, the greater the risk.

Lesson 91: Get on the Train

Thomas Edison was a historical, flesh-and-blood figure; he was born on February 11, 1847, in Milan, Ohio, and died on October 18, 1931, in West Orange, New Jersey. But he also was and remains an icon of American popular culture, one of a small pantheon of such icons. Consider this: An *icon* is a symbol rich in meaning and suggestion but short on specific detail. Few of us can fill so much as five minutes retelling the life story of George Washington, but most of us remember something about his chopping down a cherry tree or maybe even throwing a silver dollar across the Potomac. To most, Ben Franklin is little more than a picture of a wide-eyed boy entering colonial Philadelphia with two puffy bread rolls under his arms and one in his hand, or maybe he's just a man flying a kite in a thunderstorm. Theodore Roosevelt? A stocky guy with a big mustache charging up San Juan Hill. Babe Ruth? A sad-faced ball player solemnly raising his bat to indicate the spot in the stands where he intended to send the next home-run ball.

And then there is Thomas Edison. Everyone knows he "invented the light bulb," and some remember the phonograph, too. But many of us also see a mental picture of Edison as a boy, demonstrating his ambition and entrepreneurial genius in early life by selling newspapers on a train—and not only selling them, but printing them on that train as well. This is the subject of memorable scenes in the 1940 film *Young Tom Edison*, starring Mickey Rooney, but it was also the stuff of folklore before the movie, and it has remained so ever since—an image that is the property of the collective American consciousness.

It also happens to be an image attached to a true story.

Some time after November 21, 1859, the date on which the Grand Trunk Western Railway completed its lines from Toronto to Detroit via young Edison's Michigan hometown of Port Huron, the boy wrung from his overly protective mother permission to work on the train as a newsboy—a "news butcher" or "news butch." He was most active at this, his first career, traveling between Port Huron and Detroit, during the early years of the Civil War. It was a tragic time for the nation, of course, but a most opportune time to be a purveyor of news. People riding between Port Huron and Detroit wanted news, and young Edison intended to profit by giving it to them.

A stroke of born genius?

Not exactly. In becoming a news butch, Edison joined a movement already well under way. Boys peddling papers and candy were so common on American trains by mid-century that the celebrated newspaper cartoonist Thomas Nast depicted an apparently typical scene: Nast's news butch offers, "Rock candy, rock candy, sir?" To which the passenger replies, "No, no, go away. I don't have any teeth." The news butch counters: "Gum drops, sir?" The momentum of innovative entrepreneurship was hardly the exclusive property of young Tom Edison and was, in fact, sufficiently representative of the era to be celebrated by the nation's most popular cartoonist.

At first, Edison bought papers wholesale, then retailed them en route at a profit. Soon, however, according to stories he told and retold as an adult, he collected discarded type, ink, and paper from the offices of the *Detroit Free Press,* then borrowed, salvaged, or bought a small flatbed press, which he set up in the baggage car of the train he worked. Using this equipment, he launched the weekly *Grand Trunk Herald,* available at a per-copy price or by subscription for eight cents a month.

All of this was part of the 1940 Mickey Rooney film, and, appealing as it is, the story nevertheless resounds with the hollow ring of manufactured folklore. Yet, in the summer of 1976, a team of anthropologists and archaeologists from Oakland University in Rochester, Michigan, excavated the site of Edison's boyhood home and discovered 185 pieces of type and shattered beakers stained with printer's ink. Moreover, the type was identical to that which had produced the only two surviving issues of the *Herald* (a total of twenty-four issues were published during the brief life of the paper, which spanned the first six months of 1862). So it is apparent that the boy really did publish his own newspaper—surely evidence of a unique and uniquely precocious genius.

And yet, just as the news butch phenomenon was common during this period, so the notion of the teenage journalist and pressman was hardly unique. Edison biographer Neil Baldwin reports eight teens producing commercial newspapers in Boston as early as 1846. In that same year, another eight operated out of Worcester, Massachusetts, and, during the Civil War, the number of amateur newspapers, some operated by youths no older than Edison, exploded.

Looked at in the context of history, this icon of Edison's youth, celebrated in film, in lore, and in Edison's own storytelling, shrinks somewhat, and the boy Edison comes to seem something less of an original prodigy and more like a lad who simply knew a good thing when he saw it—an admirable talent, but hardly a divine gift. But if the mythic view is falsely puffed by leaving out history, so the historical view is misleadingly diminished if we ignore the two key differences that set Edison's *Herald* apart from the products of other amateur journalists.

First: In contrast to the others, Edison did not simply copy pieces from other papers and periodicals. Along with the war news, which he did gather from the commercial press, Edison printed "Local Intelegence" (his spelling)—unique stories from the immediate territory of the Grand Trunk and its passengers.

Second: It was Edison's idea—apparently truly unique—to print the paper on a moving train. This novelty not only appealed to his captive passenger–customers (at the peak of production, the *Herald* had five hundred paid subscriptions, and Edison sold an additional two hundred individual papers per trip), it eliminated downtime, allowing Edison to produce and sell almost simultaneously.

Once these two differences are taken into account, Edison's *Herald* again strikes us as the work of a prodigy. Yet, if you look closely, you can glimpse in Edison's early experience as a news butch not so much an example of early genius as a foreshadow of mature method.

As an inventor, Thomas Edison never set out to be a prodigy, a preternatural genius, a lone wolf, or a Prometheus. He sought trends, whether in the marketplace or in technology, and he engaged those trends, making the often relatively minor adjustments to them that thrust him to the very forefront of the trend. Picture a trend as a train. Edison never hesitated to board, but only *after* he got on with everyone else did he endeavor to find the very best seat.

The method of the mature Edison, inventor of modern life, was the method of the young Edison, news butch on the Grand Trunk.

Creativity does not require going against the grain or walking in the opposite direction from the crowd, let alone deliberately turning away from a productive movement. On the contrary, creativity is enhanced by the momentum of a well-established technology or the energy of an already active market. What we think of as unattainable genius may actually be no more than a modest step beyond ordinary creativity. The mechanic says, *If it ain't broke, don't fix it.* The inventor says, *If it ain't broke, fix it anyway.* The most creative position to assume is that any existing movement, any existing technology, any existing market can be made more vigorous, more efficient, and more profitable. But first, get on the train.

Lesson 92: To Innovate, Imitate

Edison obtained his first patent—U.S. Patent 90,646—on June 1, 1869, for an automatic vote recorder. This was an electrochemical device intended to record votes in such organizations as federal, state, and local legislatures. The machine consisted of the names of each legislator in metal type alongside two columns, one for "no," the other for "yes." As the legislator voted by moving a switch to the yes or no position, a recording clerk would place a sheet of chemically treated paper over the type with his name, run a metal roller over the paper, and the current would decompose the chemicals, recording the vote in the yes or no column. The process was repeated for each vote cast, and the totals were automatically tallied on a pair of dials—one for yes, the other for no—incorporated into the machine.

Years of Edison lore have depicted this as an original invention that was successful insofar as it did what it was supposed to do, but a failure insofar as no legislature ever adopted it. The problem was that it worked *too* well. It was certainly faster and more efficient than the traditional roll call process. Edison had assumed that speed and efficiency were absolute values that everyone in every profession wanted. Had he actually studied his intended market, however, he would have discovered that legislators used the time-consuming roll call process to garner last-minute votes. They did not want speed and efficiency.

It all makes for an appealing story—and the last part, about the consequences of failing to research the market, is even true. But was the automatic vote recorder an original invention?

Hardly.

Edison was inspired to create it by an article he read in *The Telegrapher*, which described various vote recording devices then under consideration by the New York State legislature as well as the city council of Washington, D.C. Moreover, the device was of interest to *The Telegrapher* because it was closely related to electrochemical recording devices used in various automatic telegraphs. Edison not only innovated on existing technology, he imitated actual emerging devices. What he produced was by no means wholly original, but it had to be only sufficiently original to merit a patent. And that it did.

Don't shun the bandwagon on principle. Be as original as you need to be, but originality is rarely a profitable goal for its own sake. Of course, even a well-populated bandwagon can be headed in the wrong direction. Make sure that whatever you imitate is worth imitating.

Lesson 93: Do It Better

Thomas Edison was not the only electric light experimenter to realize that the glowing filament of the electric lamp had to burn in a vacuum to avoid the rapidly destructive effects of oxidation. He emulated others in using a pump to evacuate the bulb, but he decided that the better the vacuum the longer the filament would burn. Unlike most of his competitors, he had a laboratory workshop so well equipped and so well staffed that he could afford to take the time to develop superb vacuum pump technology that far surpassed the prevailing state of the art. This represented no original principle or profound advance on existing principles, but it did give him the winning edge for developing a commercially viable electric light.

Profitable innovation can mean simply doing a familiar, common, proven thing better than it has ever been done before.

Lesson 94: Create by Analogy

By dictionary definition, a *prodigy* is someone with exceptional talents or powers. The adjectival form of the word—*prodigious*—describes something enormous, something great in size, force, or extent. With 1,093 patents to his name, Thomas Edison was nothing if not a *prodigious prodigy*. It is not just the sheer volume of

Edison's creativity that is so daunting, it is also its range. Electric lighting, electric power, the phonograph, motion pictures, improvements to the telegraph and telephone, pioneering work in the domestic cultivation of rubber, in the creation of plastics, in the production of an improved artificial cement—the list goes on and on in a multitude of fields, many seemingly unrelated.

Edison himself relished the image of prodigious creativity in a multitude of fields, as if he were some latter-day alchemist, and it was an essential feature of his method never to let even the most fleeting idea escape unrecorded. Indeed, few ideas escaped at least some degree of development. However, most of his apparently unrelated projects actually grew out of a small number of larger interests. The field that most powerfully held his attention from the very beginning of his inventing career was communications, and many of his patents directly concern improvements in telegraphy and, later, refinements of the telephone. But it is also apparent that the phonograph and the technology of motion pictures are intimately related to communications, as is another rather obscure invention that Edison nevertheless succeeded in profitably commercializing.

On March 13, 1876, the inventor filed for a patent on an "Improvement in Autographic Printing." The electric pen—that's what Edison called it—was a portable device that used a small reciprocating electric motor to drive a needle very rapidly up and down in order to perforate paper stencils for the reproduction of documents and drawings. The device was designed so that it could be used as freely as a conventional pen, and the motor was designed to space the tiny perforations sufficiently to prevent tearing the paper, but closely enough to make a stencil that could be used to produce a clear copy. Edison also created a specially designed frame to hold the stencil and to make both inking (using castor oil–impregnated inks of his own formulation) and printing easier.

The business world greeted the electric pen as a true innovation, and Edison profited handsomely from it before he sold the patent to Western Electric. That corporation later reverted the rights to Edison, who then sold them to the A. B. Dick Company, the firm that developed the mimeograph, the stencil-based technology that dominated business duplicating before the proliferation of economical photocopying in the early 1970s.

Edison had developed the electric pen to exploit what he thought of as a niche market and ended up laying the foundation for an important business-machine industry. He arrived at this "new" idea by extending his thinking about the cutting-edge technology of communications as well as by developing analogies with very old technologies. His patent application for the electric pen is rife with references to traditional embroidery and to the use of stencils—called "cartoons"—by the fresco painters of the Renaissance: These painters would outline a design on special paper, perforate the paper along the lines, apply the paper to an area of the fresco, then tap the design with a cloth bag (called a "pounce") filled with very fine charcoal powder. The charcoal would filter out of the bag, penetrate the perforations on the paper, and be deposited on the wall or ceiling to be painted. The result was an outline drawing.

Analogy was of the essence in Edison's creative method. It allowed him to innovate at will, because he did not have to wait hopefully for the inspiration that might or might not come, for the chance that genius might suddenly spark something out of thin air. Instead, he continually mined the past—his own, as well as the great pool of the past open to all—and he innovated by analogy based on the past.

Without a doubt, the electric pen is one of Edison's minor inventions, notwithstanding that it was immediately profitable and also gave rise to the more enduring technology of the mimeograph—not to mention the modern electric tattooing pen. Of more significance, though, was the way in which Edison, having invented the electric pen via analogy, used it in turn as an analogy by which he began to think about the acoustic replication of sound, including human speech.

Having invented the electric pen, he next began working on what he called the "speaking telegraph," which was in large part an attempt to improve on Alexander Graham Bell's brand-new telephone (patented in 1876). Edison did succeed in greatly improving the telephone by means of the so-called carbon button transmitter, which remained the unchallenged basis of the telephone transmitter and receiver for about a hundred years. But even more important was the speaking telegraph, which used the electric pen technology as the basis for a device to record telephone transmissions. This idea, in turn, morphed—by further analogy—into one of Edison's truly civilization-altering inventions, the phonograph, which used a pen-like stylus to record, preserve, and reproduce sound itself.

> Analogy is a powerful tool for creativity, and it is absolutely indispensable for faking genius. Real genius may be defined as an ability to create something from nothing. Few human beings can do this. Fortunately, the *appearance* of genius, as well as the utility and benefits of genius, can be achieved by practically anyone willing to apply analogy relentlessly. Doing this does not require creating something from nothing, it merely calls for translating one thing into something else. To develop the habit of analogy is to develop the ability to create on demand, which means the consistent and reliable ability to extend the past (reality as it happens to be) into the future (reality as you want it to be).

Lesson 95: Make the Problem the Solution

Since the appearance of Edison's most famous invention, the incandescent electric lamp, in 1879, generations have waxed poetic about how the Wizard of Menlo Park vanquished the darkness and mastered a hitherto ineluctable fact of creation, the separation of day from night.

Edison himself did nothing to discourage those who painted him as a wizard. Such a picture was good for business and attracted much-needed investment capital. But he never made the mistake of believing his own press. He knew the incandescent electric lamp was neither a poem written against darkness nor a miracle of biblical proportion. For him, the invention was not a quantum leap of inspirational genius, but merely a step—albeit *the right step*—in solving a problem he had carefully defined.

The truth is that Thomas Edison did not invent electric lighting. At the beginning of the nineteenth century—in 1806, four decades before Edison was born—the distinguished British scientist Sir Humphry Davy presented to the empire's most prestigious scientific organization, the Royal Society, a literally dazzling demonstration of electric light. He had cobbled together a device consisting of two charcoal rods wired to banks of sulfuric acid batteries. When the rods were drawn close to one another, a brilliant spark bridged the gap between the rods in a sizzling, hissing arc.

Davy had invented the electric arc light, and the members of the Royal Society were, doubtless, duly impressed. But did this device illuminate the world? No. In fact, it was of no practical, commercial value. The batteries were unwieldy, hazardous, and quickly exhausted. As for the charcoal rods, they rapidly burned away. Even if an alternative source of power could be found—and in 1806 there was none—the life of the charcoal rods was limited to a matter of hours, even minutes.

Yet others did pursue Davy's invention, and when practical electric generators began to appear in the 1860s and 1870s, a number of inventors patented arc lamps. They were at best marginally practical. Their light was brilliant, but blindingly so, making them useful in such applications as searchlights; indoors, however, where light was needed most, they were useless. The searing arc light could not be regulated, dimmed, or controlled. Besides, although hard-compacted carbon rods were an improvement over Davy's soft charcoal, they were still quite speedily consumed, making maintenance of arc lamps both labor-intensive and costly.

Still, it seemed obvious to many inventors that electric lighting had a future. Thomas Edison was just one of that crowd. Rather than working in the splendid isolation that is the romanticized image of the creative genius, he always kept his eyes open, looked around, and took a profound interest in the ways others did things and addressed problems.

One day in 1878, he visited the workshop of William Wallace. A brass and copper founder by trade, Wallace was an inventor by avocation and had been working on an electric arc lamp system with the help of a full-time electrical inventor named Moses Farmer. Edison knew that Wallace and Farmer did not have a revolutionary approach to the arc lamp, but what he came to see was the generator system they had built to power their lamps—eight of them, in a row, all at once. Now *that*, Edison concluded, was remarkable. No one before had developed a generator sufficiently powerful and efficient to do this.

Edison was impressed but not dazzled. Instead, he was moved to action. As he explained to a reporter for the *New York Sun* just one month after his visit to the Wallace workshop: "I saw for the first time everything in practical operation. It was all before me. I saw the thing had not gone so far but that I had a chance. I saw that what had been done had never been made practically useful. The intense light had not been subdivided so that it could be brought into private houses."

In five sentences spoken to a reporter, Edison related the moment that inspired the creation of what is surely one of humankind's seminal technologies. Let's take that moment apart—*reverse engineer* the great inspirational event.

To begin with, we encounter disappointment. Not Edison's disappointment, but our own. In this moment of inspiration there is no poetry, no ecstatic shout of *Eureka!* Instead, there is a conventional observation, matter-of-fact to the point of dullness: "I saw for the first time everything in practical operation. It was all before me."

Just what was "before" Edison? Eight arc lamps powered by a single generator.

Which meant—what, exactly?

Actually, it meant nothing relating *directly* to the technology of electric light. What was "all before me" was not *the* solution to the problem of electric light. We know that because of the next two sentences: "I saw the thing had not gone so far but that I had a chance. I saw that what had been done had never been made practically useful." These two sentences somewhat contradict the first sentence: "I saw for the first time everything in practical operation." If this first sentence were left standing on its own, it would mean that Wallace and Farmer had solved the problem, had invented a practical electric light. But, Edison recognized, they had not. Not by a long shot.

Even as he saw everything in practical operation, Edison also realized that "the thing" had not gone all the way. Edison the inventor still "had a chance." Wallace and Farmer had in operation a practical solution to producing electricity, a generator capable of energizing eight arc lamps, but that was just the point. They were still *arc lamps*, with all the shortcomings and inadequacies of the existing technology.

"I saw that what had been done had never been made practically useful," Edison said. "The intense light had not been subdivided so that it could be brought into private houses."

Here is no flash of sudden genius, no bolt of inspiration from the blue, but an almost building-block-like identification and analysis of a problem that has been only partially solved:

- A generator can power multiple lamps; this was a practical breakthrough.
- The lamps so powered are still *arc* lamps; therefore, Edison concluded that he still had a "chance" to innovate profitably.
- The light has "not been subdivided so that it could be brought into private houses."

The partial solution, the new generator, energized Edison's thinking, enabling him to move beyond what Wallace and Farmer *had* accomplished to what they had *failed* to achieve. It was in this failure that Edison saw sufficient space for an invention of his own.

Yet look again at the language of that final sentence. We are drawn immediately to a word at once pedestrian in its businesslike connotation, yet almost lyrical in its application to the subject at hand. *Subdivided* reads like a term out of some dishwater-dull legal contract. Applied to light, however, it seems suddenly magical. For who other than a genius could speak of subdividing so insubstantial an essence as light?

The question is not rhetorical. There *is* an answer. Who other than a genius could speak of subdividing light?

Answer: A truly creative businessman.

In looking at eight arc lamps illuminated by a single generator, Edison understood that what he really saw was electricity, a form of energy, being retailed like any other commodity. But if Wallace and Farmer had figured out a way to "subdivide" electric energy, they had not devised a similar subdivision of the *form* of electric energy that made electricity useful and profitable as a commodity: light. To exploit electricity as a retail commodity, Edison understood that he had to learn how to exploit light itself the same way, to subdivide *light* in order to bring it to the consumer. And so he *acted like a genius* and returned to his Menlo Park workshop to begin the tedious task of subdividing light.

Creativity does not start by formulating solutions—it starts by defining problems. You don't need the spark of genius. You do need the kernel of the problem: its simplest statement. Identify it, think about it, talk through it, and it will, astoundingly, become the seed of the solution you seek.

Lesson 96: Analogy Again

Analogy was the catalyst of Edison's creativity as an innovator. At its most basic, analogy served him as the currency of understanding. In his diary, Edison noted that he generally recommended "only those books that are written by men who actually try to describe things . . . by analogy with things everybody knows."

For Edison, understanding the unknown required analogy with the known. By the same token, invention and innovation did not call for creation of something entirely new so much as the creation of an analogue to what already exists. Take motion pictures. Edison repeatedly explained that the concept of a motion picture camera was suggested to him by analogy to one of his earlier inventions, the phonograph. "I had been working for several years on my experiments for recording and reproducing sounds," he wrote late in life, "and the thought occurred to me that it should be possible to devise an apparatus to do for the eye what the phonograph was designed to do for the ear."

There was the concept! But even Edison had to admit that the realization of the analogy would be difficult, perhaps impossible. He claimed that he began his investigation of motion picture technology in 1887, when the state of photography was comparatively crude, requiring long exposures using wet plates. Fast, dry-process emulsions—let alone flexible film on celluloid—lay in the future. That is, when Edison began seriously working on the phonograph-motion picture analogy, a technology to support his innovation did not yet exist.

Indeed, all he had to give him hope that he might someday be able to make good on the analogy was his awareness of the long-known physiological phenomenon of persistence of vision—the fact that the human brain does not see a series of rapidly displayed images as a succession of discrete images, but tends to blend them smoothly together. Nor was this merely a theoretical principle for Edison. Like most other people of his time, he was familiar with a variety of eighteenth- and nineteenth-century mechanical toys that created the illusion of moving pictures by successively displaying a short series of images of various stages of movement and relying on persistence of vision to meld them together into the semblance of motion. Most familiar to Edison was the Zoetrope, a popular device he had first seen as a youth. A series of related images was pasted around a cylinder. The viewer looked at the cylinder through a slit in the device. When the cylinder was rotated, the succession of images gave the illusion of motion.

The English-born photographer Eadweard Muybridge elevated the concept of motion pictures from the realm of toys with photographic motion studies executed during 1877 and 1878. Muybridge made many studies, but the classic was the 1877 series of photographs of a trotting horse, produced to settle a wager laid by California's governor Leland Stanford, who held that all four of the trotter's hooves left the ground simultaneously, whereas his opponent believed that at least one hoof was always in contact with the ground. Muybridge set up twenty-four cameras along a racecourse. Trip wires attached to the shutter of each camera were extended across the track. When the trotter moved past, each of the shutters fired in succession, recording the progress of the horse and the exact position of its hooves. Muybridge intended his motion studies to be seen as a series of individual photographs; however, when he mounted them in a Zoetrope-like device, the result was an illusion of motion so lifelike as to suggest the actual reproduction of motion.

Muybridge provided Edison with a demonstration of the principle of persistence of vision, but it was hardly a practical technology. Edison calculated that to make a motion picture just one minute long at the rate of twelve exposures per second—the minimum that would allow persistence of vision to create a convincingly smooth illusion of motion—would require 720 separate cameras.

Clearly, Edison needed to create a *single* machine in which all the necessary exposures could be made. This would require creating a fast photosensitive emulsion on something other than a flat glass plate. Even though he had not worked out this crucial technology, Edison interrupted ongoing work to improve the phonograph so that he could, on October 8, 1888, draw up a patent caveat—a step preliminary to applying for a patent—for something he dubbed the "kinetoscope," an "instrument which does for the Eye what the phonograph does for the Ear, which is the recording and reproduction of things in motion." The caveat described a device analogous to the phonograph not only in principle and function but in mechanical design. He proposed photographing a series of images at intervals of about eight seconds, recording these images on an emulsion painted on a cylinder, so as to produce a continuous spiral of successive images. The resulting photographs would be developed, then viewed through a microscope as the cylinder was rotated. Because producing the illusion of motion required the cylinder to rotate in a precise intermittent manner, Edison drew on his experience with telegraph devices he had invented to propose a variety of mechanical movements.

Some months before he drew up his patent caveat, Edison attended a live lecture-demonstration by Muybridge, who exhibited his zoopraxiscope, a device that projected drawings based on photographs (not photographs themselves), which were painted on a revolving glass disk. Two days after the lecture, on February 27, 1888, Muybridge visited Edison in his West Orange laboratory and discussed the possibility of creating talking pictures by combining the phonograph with a photographic series. Edison proposed linking and synchronizing the kinetoscope and phonograph cylinders.

Primed by the Muybridge lecture and meeting and by his work on the phonograph, Edison turned the technical work over to a group of his laboratory workers. There were two main problems. Existing photograph emulsions were too slow—insufficiently sensitive—for recording motion. Moreover, the grain of the available emulsions was too coarse for making microscopically sized images. However, the emergence at this time of celluloid, which could be wrapped around the kinetoscope cylinder, looked promising for creating a workable substrate for the photographic emulsion.

As Edison's employees labored with emulsions and celluloid, he attended, in 1889, the Universal Exhibition in Paris. Here he encountered the work of the French physiologist Étienne-Jules Marey, who had been making his own photographic studies of animal motion. Not only did Edison obtain a copy of Marey's *Physiologie du mouvment: vol des oiseaux* (*The Physiology of Movement: Bird Flight*), he spoke at length with Marey about his photographic technique. Uninfluenced by the phonograph analogy, Marey had created a camera that used not a photosensitive cylinder but a roll of paper-based film, capable of producing a spectacular sixty frames a second.

The encounter with Marey jarred Edison into a new analogy. Conceptually, the phonograph analogy was still important—to do for the eye what the phonograph did for the ear—but mechanically, Marey's roll film shifted Edison to an analogy with his own earlier automatic telegraph, which recorded and "played back" telegraphic transmissions via a strip of paper coated with an electrochemical substance. Edison called for the manufacture of a roll of sprocketed film—a film strip with sprocket holes on the sides—which would be transported by toothed wheels, just as in his automatic telegraph. He adapted another of his earlier telegraphic innovations, a relay-controlled electromechanical escapement, to produce the intermittent motion that would allow him to take and to view photographs at ten frames per second. By the early 1890s, George Eastman's Eastman Dry Plate and Film Company had developed a celluloid film stock that could be manufactured in long, sprocketed rolls. The technology of motion picture photography and viewing was finally falling into place.

Yet Edison's process of invention by analogy was hardly complete. The close of the nineteenth century saw the emergence of various coin-operated vending machines, including coin-in-slot still photographic viewers. At this point in the development of his kinetoscope, Edison could have created a movie projector, but, instead, seizing on the existing technology and an existing retail market, he developed his machine as a coin-operated peephole viewer. When the first kinetoscopes were marketed, the response was gratifying, but their novelty rapidly wore off and sales began to go flat. To stimulate flagging sales, a group of Edison's sales agents suggested creating more interesting films, including historical scenes and even narratives—stories. A handful were produced, but even these failed to rouse much interest. As a last resort, the sales agents suggested to Edison that he develop a projection system. He was reluctant to do so, perhaps because the implied analogy of such a system was too conventional to appeal to his imagination.

Whereas the analogy to the emerging vending machine technology was new and exciting (to Edison, at least), projection was an analogy to practices long used by lecturers, who illustrated their talks with lantern slides. Perhaps that seemed old hat to Edison. Nevertheless, in precisely the year when kinetoscope sales appeared to be bottoming out, 1895, the Lumiére brothers of Paris were introducing a motion-picture projection system in their native city. Grudgingly, Edison negotiated with another inventor, Thomas Armat, to create a projection system compatible with his kinetoscope camera. In January 1896, the Edison Manufacturing Company began building the Armat projectors and supplying the motion pictures for them. Through a series of analogies, which evolved as various technologies independently developed, Edison had invented or innovated a new industry and a new mass medium.

Analogy is a powerful engine of innovation, but it can also become a cage. Conceptually, the analogy between the phonograph and motion pictures proved catalytic. As a literal mechanical model, however, the phonograph became a drag on Edison's efforts to reach beyond innovation to outright invention. Nevertheless, he had sufficient suppleness of mind to give up the mechanical aspects of the original phonograph analogy when a better analogy presented itself. Indeed, he ultimately progressed beyond two analogies: that between the phonograph and the kinetoscope, and also that between the kinetoscope and the coin-operated vending machine and photo viewer. Surprisingly, in both cases, the analogies most productive of breakthrough invention—rather than hobbled innovation—harked back to earlier technologies. The automatic telegraph was older than the phonograph, and the tradition of lectures illustrated by projected slides was much older than the emerging generation of coin-operated devices proliferating in the late nineteenth century. Analogy does not necessarily proceed chronologically. Use whatever works.

Lesson 97: Another Problem, Another Solution

During his doomed effort in the late 1880s and 1890s to perfect a commercially practical system for electromagnetically extracting iron from low-grade ore, Edison encountered a host of problems, many of which he succeeded in solving brilliantly. Among these was a difficulty with keeping grinding machinery lubricated in a very dusty environment. Edison studied the problem carefully, quickly coming to the conclusion that it was impossible to get rid of dust in an operation dedicated to grinding ore on a vast scale. The production of a great deal of dust was simply inevitable and unavoidable. Since he could not rid himself of the problem, the inventor set about doing what he had often done in the past. He looked for a way to make the problem work for him rather than against him. He designed a specially molded grease cup, which he filled with oil and which, during operation, actually blended the dust with the oil in a controlled fashion, creating a thick paste around the opening of the cup. This paste formed a natural seal that prevented the oil from escaping even as it kept excess dust from entering.

The most elegant innovations don't just fix problems, they transform them into solutions.

Lesson 98: New Wholes from Old Parts

The electric lighting system that Edison developed, including the lamp, generator, and means of distribution, necessarily drew on many existing devices for models and inspiration. This presented potential patent problems, which Edison addressed by hiring an expert, Francis Upton, to research all relevant British and American patents potentially bearing on the Edison system. Upton's conclusion was telling: "I feel sure that the total you have is new, no matter if parts have been used before."

> Invention and innovation are daunting to the point of creative paralysis if one is convinced that every aspect of a complex system must be invented anew. Genuine originality relies more on the innovative manipulation and assembly of existing principles and components than it does on the absolute necessity of a new genesis for every step forward.

Lesson 99: Better to Elaborate Than Replace?

From the beginning of his work on electric lighting, Edison saw the actual incandescent lamp—the invention for which he would become most famous—as only one part of an entire electric lighting system. Of equal importance were the generator and the means of distribution; however, he put the first priority on the lamp, since that was the element that would do the most to create the market demand for the rest of the system. It was also the element that required the greatest degree of original innovation. Initially, it seemed to Edison that existing designs for generators could be readily adapted for his purposes, but while people had been using electric arc lights for many years, no incandescent electric lamp—suitable for indoor use—yet existed.

Edison was grateful for any shortcut he could take in creating his system; however, after exhaustive experimentation with the chief existing generator design candidate, he decided that it would not serve his purposes. Instead of embarking on his own research immediately, he acquired other dynamo designs and tested them all. Only when none proved to be a standout did he devote resources to creating his own design.

An inventor and innovator needs to possess two items of knowledge above all others: he needs to know what he knows and know what he does not know. Edison quickly realized that he needed to know much more about existing generator designs, and for that reason set out to study all of the available types. At first, he tried to do library research, but soon concluded that he was better off analyzing the machines themselves, close up. In effect, Edison engaged in a process of reverse engineering, dismantling and rebuilding existing machines until he understood what they could do—and what they could be made to do better. Based on this work, he drew up designs for his own generators.

Begin with the known and the available. Test these to the very limits of your intended application. To the degree that the known and the available are sufficient for your needs, use them. To the degree that they do not meet your needs, bridge the gaps by modification. To the degree that the gaps prove unbridgeable, create new designs.

Lesson 100: Prefer Evolution to Revolution

It is tempting to describe Thomas Edison's major inventions—the incandescent electric lamp, the phonograph, motion picture technology—as revolutionary, and if the term *revolutionary* is intended to describe the effect such inventions had on society and civilization, the description is appropriate enough. However, as an inventor and innovator, Edison tended to work along evolutionary rather than revolutionary lines.

His favorite invention, the phonograph, began with the notion of recording telephone messages. Why would it be important to record such messages? Edison, like other experimenters of the period, thought of the telephone as a species of telegraph—a "talking telegraph," as it was usually called at the time—and because conventional telegraph messages were always recorded, it stood to reason that users of the telephone would want a record of their messages as well. Only as Edison experimented with telegraphic recording devices (the automatic telegraph) and telephone recording devices did the idea of recording sound for its own sake evolve in his imagination. Nevertheless, his first designs for the phonograph drew on both telephone and telegraph technology. The application was revolutionary, but the concept as well as the technology were strictly evolutionary, outgrowths of an existing paradigm (telegraph messages exist to be recorded; therefore "talking telegraph" messages must be recorded) as well as existing and emerging technologies.

These days, we often have a knee-jerk reaction against "old paradigms," as if what has worked in the past must, of necessity, be rejected for the future. Edison knew better than to discard either the past or the present. He innovated upon elements of both, creating revolutionary devices through evolutionary thinking.

Lesson 101: Make the New Familiar

Most people would agree that the incandescent electric light was Edison's iconic achievement as well as his single most important invention, but Edison never considered it a stand-alone device. As Edison conceived it, whatever else it was, cheap electric indoor lighting was a reason to transform whole cities (and, later, the countryside as well) into a set of customers for a brand new business: the electric power industry.

The mere availability of electric lighting would create, Edison believed, a universal demand for electric power. Yet even Edison realized that such an extensive installation of infrastructure would require an ambitious exercise in mass marketing. His approach was to use the existence of a familiar infrastructure as a royal road to the new. The electrification of lower Manhattan—Edison's first great power project—would be entirely analogous to the existing infrastructure that supplied gas, for gas lighting and cooking, to the city. The power generating plants would be something new on the urban landscape, but the distribution of power would be through mains quite similar to those that already distributed gas. Edison even proposed to use existing gas pipes in buildings as conduits through which to run his wires, and he would replace existing gas lamp mantles with electric lighting fixtures. As for retailing his service, Edison created electric meters, which delivered the accounting functionality of long-familiar gas meters.

The analogy with the existing gas lighting infrastructure not only pushed Edison's process of innovation along, it paved the way for public acceptance of the transition from gas to electricity—a radical, civilization-altering transformation that nevertheless required remarkably few technological or cultural adaptations.

Use the familiar to think through to the new. Create new markets via familiar paths.

Lesson 102: Work Beyond the Cutting Edge

Thomas Edison is rarely described as a scientist. He was an inventor, most comfortable and most productive working within the margins—albeit the outer margins—of what was well known and well established. Yet his long involvement in the technology of transforming one form of energy into another—electricity into light and sound, heat into steam and steam into electric current—drove him beyond the cutting edge on at least one occasion.

During the 1880s, Edison proposed to produce electricity directly from coal using what he called a pyromagnetic generator. As an inventor of devices to convert energy, Edison was eager to find the most direct means of producing the form of energy he most often exploited: electricity. His enemy was entropy, the dissipation of useful energy as useless heat inherent in the process of creating steam to power a turbine to drive a generator to produce electric power. Eliminate as many of the mechanical and intermediate steps intervening in the transfer of one form of energy into another, and the production of electricity could be cheap and plentiful.

Inspired by the example of his favorite scientist, the Englishman Michael Faraday, who had been deeply involved in the investigation of the convertibility of forces, Edison followed up on a phenomenon he had observed when anthracite carbon (in the form of a coke rod) and a strip of metal were heated to incandescence in a vessel into which a gas vapor was injected. The gas would ionize, setting up an electrical current.

The pyromagnetic generator was but one aspect of Edison's growing interest in the convertibility of forces. However, the device proved dangerously explosive, and Edison abandoned it. Nevertheless, he had come tantalizingly close to penetrating the surface of energy conversion, but was never able to commercialize an invention that would produce electricity directly from coal or any other substance.

Because Edison's experiments in the convertibility of forces produced no practical result—certainly no invention—they have been largely ignored. Nevertheless, devices such as his pyromagnetic generator should serve as an inspiration for all innovators to extend their reach well beyond their grasp. Edison never regretted his boldest experiments.

Appendix One

AN EDISON CHRONOLOGY

1847

February 11: Thomas Alva Edison is born in Milan, Ohio.

1859-1860

Winter: Young Tom Edison goes to work as a "news butcher," selling newspapers, magazines, dime novels, candy, and other sundries on the trains of the Grand Trunk Western Railway between Port Huron and Detroit.

1862

Spring: Edison writes, edits, publishes, and sells *The Weekly Herald* aboard a Grand Trunk train.

Fall: Edison apprentices to telegrapher James Mackenzie, station agent at Mount Clemens, Michigan.

1864-1865

Fall–winter: While working as a telegrapher for Western Union in Indianapolis, Indiana, Edison commences research to improve telegraph repeaters and embarks on design work for telegraphy devices that would enable the simultaneous transmission and reception of multiple telegraph messages along a single line.

1868

March–April: Edison moves to Boston, where he works in the main office of Western Union and makes valuable financial and technical contacts.

October 13: Edison applies for a patent on his electric vote recorder.

January 30: Resigning from Western Union, Edison becomes a full-time inventor and telegraph entrepreneur.

April–May: Edison leaves Boston for New York City, the nation's financial capital.

1870

February 10–15: The Gold and Stock Telegraph Company finances the Newark Telegraph Works, in Newark, New Jersey, Edison's first major laboratory–workshop.

1871

October: Mary Stilwell joins Edison's News Reporting Telegraph Company (Newark) as an employee. Edison and Stilwell marry on Christmas day.

1872

December 14: The Automatic Telegraph Company begins operations. Edison tests automatic telegraph service between New York City, Washington, D.C., and Charleston, South Carolina.

1873

February 18: Marion Estelle Edison, nicknamed "Dot," is born in Newark.

August 2: Edison draws up a patent caveat for the quadruplex telegraph, which would enable the simultaneous transmission and reception of four messages over a single line.

1874

April 10: While working on electrochemical recording technology, Edison discovers what he calls the "electromotograph phenomenon," electrochemical reactions that either reduce or increase friction. The discovery will influence innovations in electric relays and telephone technology.

Summer: Edison develops the electric-pen copying system.

October 30: Edison draws up a patent caveat to cover a facsimile telegraph system, which would transmit pictures by wire.

November 22: Edison prepares a caveat on an acoustic-telegraph system, an invention related to the telephone. During this period he also takes note of what he calls the "etheric force," later identified as high-frequency electromagnetic waves. Although Edison pursues investigations of this phenomenon, he makes no practical use of what others will later harness as the basis of radio.

1876

January 10: Thomas Alva Edison Jr., nicknamed "Dash," is born in Newark.

March: Edison patents his improved electric-pen copying system.

March 26–28: The Edison family and the Edison laboratory move to Menlo Park, New Jersey.

October 30: Edison patents the reciprocating tuning fork motor.

1877

January 20: Edison conducts his first experiments on what will become the carbon button telephone transmitter—a key innovation in modern telephony—patented on April 18.

July 17–18: After sketching out a telephone message recorder and repeater, Edison draws plans for the phonograph.

On or about September 10: Edison begins experimenting with incandescent electric lighting.

December 1–6: Edison experimenter and shop craftsman John Kruesi transforms the inventor's drawings into the first cylinder phonograph, which Edison demonstrates for *Scientific American* the following day. He applies for a patent on December 15.

1878

February 19: Edison secures his first phonograph patent.

April 10: The *New York Graphic* coins the phrase "Wizard of Menlo Park" to describe Thomas Edison.

April 19: The tasimeter principle is first presented publicly—a device for electrically measuring temperature with great accuracy.

September 10: Edison draws up his first caveat covering electric lighting. Days later, he announces to the press that he has "solved the problem" of incandescent electric lighting.

October 5: Edison applies for his first electric lighting patent.

October 26: William Leslie Edison is born in Menlo Park, New Jersey.

November 29–30: As part of his electric lighting system, Edison designs the world's first electric meter—making it possible to bill electric consumers for power used.

December 3: Edison applies for a patent on an electric generator that uses the tuning-fork engine technology he had developed earlier. Throughout December, he works on generator designs.

1879

January 2: Edison starts to build his first major generator.

January 19–29: In search of the best filament for his electric light, Edison conducts exhaustive tests on a vast array of materials.

December 9: Convinced that he can economically separate commercial-grade iron from low-grade ore using an electromagnetic process, Edison creates the Edison Ore Milling Company.

December 31: Edison publicly demonstrates his electric lighting system at Menlo Park.

1880

February 13: Edison discovers the "Edison Effect," the flow of electric current not only through the filament of his electric light, but through the vacuum of the bulb itself. To measure this flow, Edison inserted a third electrode into the bulb and attached it to a meter. The inventor could think of no practical application for the "Edison Effect," but, later, in other hands, it became the basis of the electron—or vacuum—tube, the foundation of radio and other electronic technologies.

May 13: Edison tests a small electric railway at Menlo Park.

July 3: *Science* magazine, financed by Edison, publishes its first number on this date.

October 1: Commercial manufacture of electric lamps begins at Menlo Park.

1881

July 26: Edison successfully patents a facsimile telegraph system.

September: Edison demonstrates his magnetic ore separator at Quonocontaug, Rhode Island.

1882

September 4: The Pearl Street generating station opens in lower Manhattan.

November: Edison closes the Menlo Park workshop–laboratory complex and opens facilities in New York City.

1884

August 9: Mary Stilwell Edison, the inventor's wife, dies at Menlo Park.

1886

January: Edison buys Glenmont, in Llewellyn Park, New Jersey, which becomes his home.

February 24: Edison marries Mina Miller.

1887

December: Edison opens a new laboratory–workshop complex in West Orange, New Jersey.

1888

May 31: Madeleine Edison is born.

July–December: Edison begins experimenting with electrocution as a means of judicial execution. The result is the electric chair.

October 8: Edison drafts four patent caveats to cover the kinetoscope and kinetograph, which form the basis of motion picture technology.

1890

May–August: Edison begins iron ore separation tests at the Ogden mine, Sussex County, New Jersey.

August 3: Charles Edison is born.

Summer: In collaboration with writer George P. Lathrop, Edison begins work on an abortive science fiction novel, a book about the future, to be called *Progress*.

1891

August 24: Edison patents the kinetoscope and kinetograph.

1892

April 15: The General Electric Company (originally associated with the Edison General Electric Company) is organized; it finances Edison's research on electric light and power.

1893

February: The "Black Maria" motion picture studio is built, becoming operational in May.

May 9: Edison exhibits his peephole kinetoscope at the Brooklyn Institute of Arts and Sciences.

1894

January: "Edison Kinetographic Record of a Sneeze," also known as "Fred Ott's Sneeze," produced by Edison employee William K. L. Dickson, becomes the first copyrighted motion picture. (Frederick Ott was the brother of John Ott, another Edison employee.) Dickson and Theodore Heise, another Edison film employee, copyright some seventy-five more movies during the year.

April 14: The Holland Brothers, 1155 Broadway, New York City, offer the first commercial exhibition of the peephole kinetoscope.

1896

January 15: Edison Manufacturing Company licenses Thomas Armat's Phantoscope, a movie projection system, to be made and marketed (with design modifications) as the Edison Vitascope. Edison motion picture technology begins a transition from peephole viewing to auditorium projection.

January: Edison commences experimentation with X-rays, also known at the time as Roentgen rays.

April 23: A Vitascope motion picture premieres commercially at Koster and Bial's Music Hall in New York City. Also during this month, Edison begins tests of a gold ore separation process.

1897

November 30: Edison's projectoscope or projecting kinetoscope—developed as a result of its inventor's dissatisfaction with the Armat projector—is first commercially demonstrated on this day.

1898

July 10: Theodore Miller Edison is born.

December: Edison becomes interested in the Portland (artificial) cement industry and tours the Lehigh Valley of Pennsylvania to observe Portland cement plants.

1899

January: Edison designs a rotary kiln of unprecedented size for the manufacture of Portland cement.

April 15: The Edison Portland Cement Company is organized.

Summer: Edison decides to improve storage battery technology with an eye toward using light, efficient batteries to power electric vehicles.

1900

September: Operations of Edison's iron ore separating plant are indefinitely suspended.

November 1: Edison shuts down gold ore experimentation.

1901

Winter: Having largely abandoned the iron and gold processing business, Edison turns to the production of Portland cement, supervising construction of the Edison Portland Cement works at Stewartsville, New Jersey, which uses as much of the costly iron ore concentrating equipment as Edison can salvage and redesign.

May 27: The Edison Storage Battery Company is organized. Although electric automobiles rapidly lose ground to gasoline-powered vehicles, Edison innovates many new uses for his greatly improved storage batteries, and the business is highly profitable.

1902

December 6: The inventor's son Thomas A. Edison Jr. sells the right to use his name to a manufacturer of a quack patent medical device known as the Magno-Electric Vitalizer. Thomas A. Edison Sr. is outraged, fearing diminishment of his trademark and reputation.

1903

January: Production of an innovative alkaline (rather than acid) storage battery begins.

December: The Edison Manufacturing Company releases *The Great Train Robbery*. Directed by Edison employee Edwin S. Porter, this landmark film is the first to embody sustained narrative—to really tell a story—and the first to employ many of the standard features of modern film making, including creative editing and point-of-view camera angles. A great commercial success, it may be considered the first truly commercial motion picture and the immediate origin of the modern film industry.

1904

October 2: Edison employee Clarence M. Dally dies horribly from radiation burns suffered during X-ray experiments. Profoundly shaken, Edison abandons all work on X-ray technology and even refuses to submit to X-ray examination by his own physicians.

1906

October: Eager to stimulate demand for Portland cement, Edison begins developing molds for the manufacture of poured concrete houses.

1908

October 1: The breakthrough Amberol phonograph cylinders are introduced, offering finer grooves that double playing time from two to four minutes.

December: Edison tightens his grip on the emerging motion picture industry by forming the Motion Picture Patents Company.

1909

July 1: A significantly improved alkaline storage battery (the "A" type) goes into production.

1910

January: Edison lays plans to create an Engineering Department in West Orange to centralize and rationalize research and development for all Edison companies. It will be the world's first formally established corporate R&D operation.

August 26: Edison demonstrates what he calls the kinetophone—"speaking pictures"—to newspapermen at his West Orange laboratory.

1912

Fall: Edison introduces the new "Blue Amberol" cylinder records even as he debuts his Diamond Disc phonograph, signaling his impending abandonment of cylinder recording and embrace of the now-dominant disc technology.

1917

April 9: The Motion Picture Patents Company's stranglehold on the U.S. film industry is broken by the Supreme Court's decision against Edison in *Motion Picture Patents Company v. Universal Film Manufacturing Company*.

1927

July: Engaged in far-ranging research to find an alternative natural source of rubber, Edison creates the Edison Botanic Research

Corporation, dedicated to formulating processes for extracting rubber from plant substances native to the United States.

1929

October 21: The nation celebrates the Golden Jubilee of Light to commemorate the invention of the incandescent electric lamp.

1931

January 6: Edison executes U.S. Patent 1,908,830, "Holder for Article to be Electroplated," his last patent.

October 18: The inventor dies at his home, Glenmont.

Appendix Two

TWO HUNDRED REPRESENTATIVE PATENTS

Representative Patents: 1869-1875

U.S. Patent 0,090,646: Electrographic Vote-Recorder
U.S. Patent 0,091,527: Printing-Telegraphs
U.S. Patent 0,111,112: Governors for Electro-Motors
U.S. Patent 0,114,656: Telegraphic Transmitting Instruments
U.S. Patent 0,124,800: Telegraphic Recording Instruments
U.S. Patent 0,126,528: Type-Wheels for Printing-Telegraphs
U.S. Patent 0,133,019: Electrical Printing-Machines
U.S. Patent 0,133,841: Type-Writing Machines
U.S. Patent 0,134,866: Printing-Telegraph Instruments
U.S. Patent 0,134,867: Automatic Telegraph Instruments
U.S. Patent 0,141,774: Chemical Telegraphs
U.S. Patent 0,142,999: Galvanic Batteries
U.S. Patent 0,147,917: Duplex Telegraphs
U.S. Patent 0,156,843: Duplex Chemical Telegraphs
U.S. Patent 0,168,242: Transmitters and Receivers for Automatic Telegraphs
U.S. Patent 0,172,305: Automatic Roman-Character Telegraphs

Representative Patents: 1876-1880

U.S. Patent 0,180,857: Autographic Printing
U.S. Patent 0,182,996: Acoustic Telegraph
U.S. Patent 0,185,507: Electro-Harmonic Multiplex Telegraphs

U.S. Patent 0,186,548: Telegraphic Alarm and Signal Apparatus

U.S. Patent 0,196,747: Stencil-Pens (later adapted as a tattoo machine)

U.S. Patent 0,198,087: Telephonic Telegraphs

U.S. Patent 0,198,089: Telephonic or Electro-Harmonic Telegraphs

U.S. Patent 0,200,521: Phonograph or Speaking Machines

U.S. Patent 0,200,993: Acoustic Telegraphs

U.S. Patent 0,200,994: Automatic-Telegraph Perforator and Transmitter

U.S. Patent 0,201,760: Speaking-Machines

U.S. Patent 0,203,013: Speaking-Telegraphs

U.S. Patent 0,203,016: Speaking-Telephones

U.S. Patent 0,203,018: Telephones or Speaking-Telegraphs

U.S. Patent 0,203,329: Perforating Pens

U.S. Patent 0,205,370: Pneumatic Stencil-Pens

U.S. Patent 0,210,767: Vocal Engines

U.S. Patent 0,214,636: Electric Lights

U.S. Patent 0,217,781: Sextuplex Telegraphs

U.S. Patent 0,219,393: Dynamo-Electric Machine

U.S. Patent 0,222,390: Carbon-Telephones

U.S. Patent 0,222,881: Magneto-Electric Machines (The Edison dynamo, nicknamed "long-legged Mary-Ann."

U.S. Patent 0,223,898: Electric Lamp (the original incandescent light bulb)

U.S. Patent 0,227,226: Safety-Conductor for Electric Lights

U.S. Patent 0,227,679: Phonograph

U.S. Patent 0,228,329: Magnetic Ore-Separator

U.S. Patent 0,230,255: Method of Manufacturing Electric Lamps

U.S. Patent 0,231,704: Electro-Chemical Receiving-Telephone

U.S. Patent 0,238,868: Manufacture of Carbons for Incandescent Electric Lamps

U.S. Patent 0,239,147: System of Electric Lighting

U.S. Patent 0,240,678: Webermeter

U.S. Patent 0,242,901: Electric Meter

U.S. Patent 0,248,425: Apparatus for Producing High Vacuums
U.S. Patent 0,248,429: Electric Motor
U.S. Patent 0,248,431: Preserving Fruit
U.S. Patent 0,248,432: Magnetic Separator

Representative Patents: 1881

U.S. Patent 0,248,435: Utilizing Electricity as a Motive Power
U.S. Patent 0,251,552: Underground Conductors
U.S. Patent 0,263,132: Electro-Magnetic Railway
U.S. Patent 0,263,142: Electrical Distribution System
U.S. Patent 0,265,775: Electric-Arc Light
U.S. Patent 0,265,778: Electro-Magnetic Railway-Engine
U.S. Patent 0,265,786: Apparatus for the Electrical Transmission
of Power

Representative Patents: 1882-1884

U.S. Patent 0,273,489: Turn-Table for Electric Railways
U.S. Patent 0,273,490: Electro-Magnetic Railway System
U.S. Patent 0,273,715: Art of Malleableizing Iron
U.S. Patent 0,278,418: Apparatus for Translating Electric Currents
From High to Low Tension
U.S. Patent 0,293,433: Insulation of Railroad-Tracks Used for
Electrical Circuits
U.S. Patent 0,295,990: Type-Writer
U.S. Patent 0,304,084: Device for Protecting Electric-Light
Systems from Lightning
U.S. Patent 0,307,029: Filament for Incandescent Lamps
U.S. Patent 0,314,115: Chemical Stock Quotation Telegraph

Representative Patents: 1885-1888

U.S. Patent 0,333,291: Way-Station Quadruplex Telegraphy
U.S. Patent 0,340,707: Telephonic Repeater
U.S. Patent 0,350,234: System of Railway Signaling

U.S. Patent 0,350,235: Railway-Telegraphy

U.S. Patent 0,370,124: Manufacture of Filaments for Incandescing Electric Lights

U.S. Patent 0,380,100: Pyromagnetic Motor

U.S. Patent 0,380,101: System of Electrical Distribution

U.S. Patent 0,393,465: Method of Preparing Phonograph Recording-Surfaces

U.S. Patent 0,393,966: Method of Recording and Reproducing Sounds

U.S. Patent 0,394,106: Phonograph-Reproducer

U.S. Patent 0,395,123: Circuit-Controller for Dynamo-Electric Machines

U.S. Patent 0,397,705: Method of Winding Field-Magnets

U.S. Patent 0,400,317: Ore-Separator

Representative Patents: 1889-1890

U.S. Patent 0,420,594: Quadruplex Telegraph

U.S. Patent 0,423,039: Phonograph for Dolls or other Toys

U.S. Patent 0,425,760: Measurement of Electricity in Distribution Systems

U.S. Patent 0,430,279: Voltaic Battery

U.S. Patent 0,434,587: Thermo-Electric Battery

U.S. Patent 0,434,588: Magnetic Ore-Separator

U.S. Patent 0,434,589: Propelling Mechanism for Electric Vehicles

U.S. Patent 0,435,687: Means for Charging and Using Secondary Batteries

U.S. Patent 0,435,688: Process of and Apparatus for Generating Electricity

U.S. Patent 0,436,127: Electric Motor

U.S. Patent 0,436,968: Method of and Apparatus for Drawing Wire

U.S. Patent 0,437,428: Propelling Device for Electric Cars

U.S. Patent 0,438,300: Gage for Testing Fibers for Incandescent-Lamp Carbons

U.S. Patent 0,438,305: Fuse-Block

U.S. Patent 0,438,309: Method of Insulating Electrical Conductors

U.S. Patent 0,446,667: Locomotive for Electric Railways

U.S. Patent 0,448,778: Electric Railway

U.S. Patent 0,448,781: Turning-Off Device for Phonographs

U.S. Patent 0,452,913: Sextuplex Telegraph

Representative Patents: 1891-1892

U.S. Patent 0,456,301: Phonograph-Doll

U.S. Patent 0,460,122: Process of and Apparatus for Generating Electricity

U.S. Patent 0,465,250: Process of Extracting Copper Pyrites

U.S. Patent 0,465,251: Method of Bricking Fine Ores

U.S. Patent 0,470,928: Alternating-Current Generator

U.S. Patent 0,474,591: Process of Extracting Gold from Sulphide Ores

U.S. Patent 0,474,592: Ore-Conveying Apparatus

U.S. Patent 0,474,593: Dust-Proof Swivel Shaft-Bearing

U.S. Patent 0,476,983: Pyromagnetic Generator

U.S. Patent 0,476,985: Trolley for Electric Railways

U.S. Patent 0,476,988: Lightning-Arrester

U.S. Patent 0,479,184: Fac-simile Telegraph

U.S. Patent 0,484,183: Electrical Depositing-Meter

U.S. Patent 0,490,953: Art of Generating Electricity

U.S. Patent 0,493,426: Apparatus for Exhibiting Photographs of Moving Objects

U.S. Patent 0,498,385: Roller for Crushing Ore or Other Material

U.S. Patent 0,506,215: Method of Making Plate Glass

U.S. Patent 0,506,216: Apparatus for Making Glass

U.S. Patent 0,509,428: Composition Brick and Method of Making Same

Representative Patents: 1893-1903

U.S. Patent 0,513,096: Method of and Apparatus for Mixing Materials

U.S. Patent 0,526,147: Art of Plating One Material with Another

U.S. Patent 0,534,208: Induction-Converter

U.S. Patent 0,543,985: Incandescent Conductor for Electric Lamps

U.S. Patent 0,543,986: Process of Treating and Products Derived from Vegetable Fibers

U.S. Patent 0,563,462: Method of and Apparatus for Drawing Wire

U.S. Patent 0,589,168: Kinetographic Camera

U.S. Patent 0,643,764: Method of Reheating Compressed Air for Industrial Purposes

U.S. Patent 0,648,934: Process of Screening or Sizing Very Fine Materials

U.S. Patent 0,648,935: Apparatus for Duplicating Phonograph-Records

U.S. Patent 0,657,527: Process of Making Metallic Duplicate Phonograph-Records

U.S. Patent 0,660,845: Apparatus for Sampling, Averaging, Mixing, and Storing Materials in Bulk

U.S. Patent 0,661,238: Machine for Forming Pulverized Material into Briquets

U.S. Patent 0,672,616: Method of Breaking Rock

U.S. Patent 0,672,617: Apparatus for Breaking Rock

U.S. Patent 0,674,057: Grinding or Crushing Rolls

U.S. Patent 0,678,722: Reversible Galvanic Battery

U.S. Patent 0,721,870: Funnel for Filling Storage-Battery Cans or Analogous Purposes

U.S. Patent 0,722,502: Means for Handling Cable-Drawn Cars on Inclines

U.S. Patent 0,724,089: Means for Operating Motors in Dust-Laden Atmospheres

U.S. Patent 0,734,522: Process of Nickel-Plating

U.S. Patent 0,750,102: Electrical Automobile

Representative Patents: 1904-1909

U.S. Patent 0,754,756: Process of Separating Ores from Magnetic Gangue

U.S. Patent 0,759,356: Method of Burning Portland-Cement Clinker, & c.

U.S. Patent 0,759,357: Apparatus for Burning Portland-Cement Clinker & c.

U.S. Patent 0,764,183: Method of Separating Mechanically-Entrained Globules from Gases

U.S. Patent 0,766,815: Primary Battery

U.S. Patent 0,767,216: Apparatus for Vacuously Depositing Metals

U.S. Patent 0,767,554: Method of Rendering Storage-Battery Gases Non-Explosive

U.S. Patent 0,772,647: Photographic Film for Moving-Picture Machines

U.S. Patent 0,772,648: Vehicle-Wheel

U.S. Patent 0,775,600: Rotary Cement-Kiln

U.S. Patent 0,785,297: Gas-Separator for Storage Batteries

U.S. Patent 0,802,631: Apparatus for Burning Portland-Cement Clinker

U.S. Patent 0,821,625: Process of Treating Alkaline Storage Batteries

U.S. Patent 0,821,628: Process for Making Conducting-Films

U.S. Patent 0,827,089: Calcining-Furnace

U.S. Patent 0,832,046: Automatic Weighing and Mixing Apparatus

U.S. Patent 0,847,746: Electrical Welding Apparatus

U.S. Patent 0,850,881: Composite Metal

U.S. Patent 0,850,912: Process of Making Articles by Electroplating

U.S. Patent 0,855,562: Diaphragm for Talking-Machines

U.S. Patent 0,861,241: Portland Cement and Process of Manufacturing the Same

U.S. Patent 0,865,367: Fluorescent Electric Lamp

U.S. Patent 0,879,859: Apparatus for Producing Very Thin Sheet Metal

U.S. Patent 0,909,167: Waterproofing-Paint for Portland-Cement Buildings

U.S. Patent 0,909,168: Waterproofing Fibers and Fabrics

U.S. Patent 0,939,992: Phonographic Recording and Reproducing Machine

U.S. Patent 0,941,630: Process and Apparatus for Artificially Aging or Seasoning Portland Cement

U.S. Patent 0,943,663: Horn for Talking-Machines

Representative Patents: 1910–1915

U.S. Patent 0,950,227: Apparatus for Making Metallic Films or Flakes

U.S. Patent 0,964,097: Device for Viewing Moving Pictures

U.S. Patent 0,967,178: Tube-Forming Machine

U.S. Patent 0,970,616: Flying-Machine

U.S. Patent 1,016,874: Means and Method for Preventing Depletion of [Battery] Electrolyte

U.S. Patent 1,050,629: Art of Separating Copper from Other Metals

U.S. Patent 1,059,661: Manufacture of Portland Cement

U.S. Patent 1,083,355: Art of Forming Chemical Compounds

U.S. Patent 1,106,444: Fuel-Feeding Apparatus

U.S. Patent 1,123,261: Mold for Concrete Construction

U.S. Patent 1,138,360: Method of Presenting the Illusion of Scenes in Colors

U.S. Patent 1,143,818: Charging Storage Batteries

U.S. Patent 1,148,832: Means for Utilizing the Waste Heat in Kilns

U.S. Patent 1,178,062: Moving-Picture Apparatus

Representative Patents: 1916-1931

- U.S. Patent 1,182,897: Apparatus for Recording and Reproducing Motion and Sounds
- U.S. Patent 1,192,400: Electrical System for Automobiles
- U.S. Patent 1,219,272: Process of Constructing Concrete Buildings
- U.S. Patent 1,255,517: Starting and Current-Supplying System for Automobiles
- U.S. Patent 1,266,778: Process of Making Screens for Projection
- U.S. Patent 1,275,232: Production of Finely-Divided Metals
- U.S. Patent 1,323,218: Method and Means for Improving the Rendition of Musical Compositions
- U.S. Patent 1,326,854: Apparatus for the Production of Concrete Structure
- U.S. Patent 1,342,326: Composition of Matter for Sound-Records or the Like and Process of Making the Same
- U.S. Patent 1,371,414: Nickel-Plating
- U.S. Patent 1,379,089: Production of Thin Metallic Sheets or Foils
- U.S. Patent 1,495,580: Method of Producing Chlorinated Rubber
- U.S. Patent 1,678,246: Production of Alkali-Metal Compounds from Silicates Containing Them
- U.S. Patent 1,702,935: Receiving Apparatus for Radio and Telephone Circuits
- U.S. Patent 1,740,079: Extraction of Rubber from Plants
- U.S. Patent 1,744,534: Production of Molded Articles
- U.S. Patent 1,908,830: Holder for Article to be Electroplated

Appendix Three

SUGGESTED READING

Web Sites

IEEE Virtual Museum, "Wizard in Training": www.ieee-virtual-museum.org/exhibit/exhibit.php?id=159253&lid=1

Lemelson Center, "Edison Invents!": http://invention.smithsonian.org/centerpieces/edison/default.asp.

Rutgers University, "Thomas A. Edison Papers": http://edison.rutgers.edu.

Books

Baldwin, Neil. *Edison: Inventing the Century*. New York: Hyperion, 1995.

Bazerman, Charles. *The Languages of Edison's Light*. Cambridge, Mass.: MIT Press, 1999.

Collins, Theresa M., and Lisa Gitelman. *Thomas Edison and Modern America: A Brief History with Documents*. New York: Beford/St. Martin's, 2002.

Conot, Robert. *A Streak of Luck*. New York: Seaview Press, 1979.

Dyer, Frank L., and Thomas C. Martin, with William H. Meadowcroft. *Edison: His Life and Inventions*, 2 vols. New York: HarperCollins, 1910; rev. ed. 1929.

Essig, Mark. *Edison and the Electric Chair: A Story of Light and Death*. New York: Walker, 2003.

Friedel, Robert, and Paul Israel, with Bernard S. Finn. *Edison's Electric Light: Biography of an Invention*. New Brunswick, N.J.: Rutgers University Press, 1986.

Gitelman, Lisa. *Scripts, Grooves, and Writing Machines: Representing Technology in the Edison Era*. Stanford, Calif.: Stanford University Press, 1999.

Harvith, John, and Susan Edwards Harvith, eds. *Edison, Musicians and the Phonograph: A Century in Retrospect*. New York: Greenwood Press, 1987.

Hendricks, Gordon. *The Edison Motion Picture Myth*. Berkeley: University of California Press, 1961.

Hughes, Thomas Parke. *Networks of Power: Electrification in Western Society, 1880–1930*. Baltimore: Johns Hopkins University Press, 1983.

Israel, Paul. *Edison: A Life of Invention*. New York: Wiley, 1998.

Israel, Paul. *From Machine Shop to Industrial Laboratory: Telegraphy and the Changing Context of American Invention, 1830–1920*. Baltimore: Johns Hopkins University Press, 1992.

Jonnes, Jill. *Empires of Light: Edison, Tesla, Westinghouse, and the Rage to Electrify the World*. New York: Random House, 2003.

Josephson, Matthew. *Edison: A Biography*. New York: McGraw-Hill, 1959.

Melosi, Martin V. *Thomas A. Edison and the Modernization of America*. Glenview, Ill.: Scott, Foresman/Little, Brown Higher Education, 1990.

Millard, Andre J. *Edison and the Business of Innovation*. Baltimore: Johns Hopkins University Press, 1990.

Moran, Richard. *Executioner's Current: Thomas Edison, George Westinghouse, and the Invention of the Electric Chair*. New York: Knopf, 2002.

Musser, Charles. *Before the Nickelodeon: Edwin S. Porter and the Edison Manufacturing Company*. Berkeley: University of California Press, 1991.

Musser, Charles. *Edison Motion Pictures, 1890–1900: An Annotated Filmography*. Washington, D.C.: Smithsonian Institution Press, 1997.

Musser, Charles. *The Emergence of Cinema: The American Screen to 1907*. Berkeley: University of California Press, 1990.

Musser, Charles. *Thomas A. Edison and His Kinetographic Motion Pictures*. New Brunswick, N.J.: Rutgers University Press for the Friends of Edison National Historic Site, 1995.

Newton, James D. *Uncommon Friends: Life with Thomas Edison, Henry Ford, Harvey Firestone, Alexis Carrel and Charles Lindbergh*. San Diego: Harcourt, Brace, Jovanovich, 1987.

Pretzer, William S., ed. *Working at Inventing: Thomas Edison and the Menlo Park Experience*. Dearborn, Mich.: Henry Ford Museum & Greenfield Village, 1989; reprint edition, Baltimore: Johns Hopkins University Press, 2002.

Read, Oliver, and Walter L. Welch. *From Tin Foil to Stereo: The Evolution of the Phonograph*. Indianapolis: Sams, 1976.

Runes, Dagobert D., ed. *The Diary and Sundry Observations of Thomas Alva Edison*. New York: Philosophical Library, 1948.

Smoot, Tom. *The Edisons of Fort Myers: Discoveries of the Heart*. Sarasota, Fla.: Pineapple Press, 2004.

Thulesius, Olav. *Edison in Florida: The Green Laboratory*. Gainesville: University Press of Florida, 1997.

Vanderbilt, Byron. *Thomas Edison, Chemist*. Washington, D.C.: American Chemical Society, 1971.

Wachhorst, Wyn. *Thomas Alva Edison: An American Myth*. Cambridge, Mass.: M.I.T. Press, 1981.

The Author

Alan Axelrod is the author of *Eisenhower on Leadership* (Jossey-Bass, 2006), *Patton: A Biography,* edited by General Wesley Clark (Palgrave Macmillan, 2006), *Getting Your Way Every Day: Mastering the Art of Pure Persuasion* (AMACOM, 2007), and *Patton on Leadership: Strategic Lessons for Corporate Warfare* (Prentice Hall, 1999), in addition to many others. He is also coeditor (with Christopher G. DePree) of *Van Nostrand's Concise Encyclopedia of Science* (Wiley, 2003).

Axelrod has served as consultant to Siemens AG (Munich, Germany), Richard E. Steele, Jr. and Associates (Atlanta, Georgia), the Goizueta School of Business, Emory University (Atlanta), and Saint Joseph's Hospital (Atlanta), as well as numerous museums and cultural institutions, including The Henry Ford (Dearborn, Michigan), the Metropolitan Museum of Art (New York City), the Strong National Museum of Play (Rochester, New York), the Airman Memorial Museum (Suitland, Maryland), and the Henry Francis du Pont Winterthur Museum (Winterthur, Delaware). Axelrod has been a creative consultant (and on-camera personality) for *The Wild West* television documentary series (Warner Bros., 1993), *Civil War Journal* (A&E Network, 1994), and The Discovery Channel, and has appeared on MSNBC, CNN, CNNfn, CNBC, and the major broadcast networks as well as many radio news and talk programs, including National Public Radio. He and his work have been featured in such magazines as *BusinessWeek*, *Fortune*, *TV Guide*, *Men's Health*, *Cosmopolitan*, *Inc.*, *Harvard Management Update*, and *Atlanta Business Chronicle*.

After receiving his Ph.D. in English (specializing in early American literature and culture) from the University of Iowa in 1979, Axelrod taught early American literature and culture at Lake Forest College (Lake Forest, Illinois) and at Furman University (Greenville, South Carolina). He then entered scholarly publishing in 1982 as associate editor and scholar with the Henry Francis du Pont Winterthur Museum, an institution specializing in the history and material culture of America prior to 1832. He was a publishing executive in New York City from 1984 to 1991 and a partner in Zenda, a creative services firm, until 1994, when he become director of development for Turner Publishing (Atlanta), a subsidiary of Turner Broadcasting System. In 1997, he founded The Ian Samuel Group, a creative services and book-packaging firm. He lives in Atlanta with his wife, Anita, and son, Ian.

Index